Praise for *Blue Labour*

'An imaginative attempt at transcending binary politics, Lord Glasman's book will make for an unsettling read for many Labour supporters [. . .] Given where the country is, and where we are heading, nothing this important is going to be easy.'
Jon Cruddas, politicshome.com

'Maurice Glasman's book is an urgent reminder that statecraft is not about immediate victories but securing well-being for all [. . .] clear, impassioned, grounded in specificities – something of a mouthwash after the sour taste of our regular current diet. For anyone who still believes we haven't missed the tide, it is a very necessary resource.'
Rowan Williams, *New Statesman*

'A slender and elegant analysis . . . Here's hoping the publisher sends a copy to each and every Labour MP for Christmas.'
Nina Power, *Compact*

'Well worth reading [. . .] a book that ranges restlessly and often enlighteningly across politics ancient and modern, economics right and left, and philosophy.'
John Lloyd, *Times Literary Supplement*

'Powerfully argues for the restoration of the bonds offered by faith, patriotism, community and family aided by a guaranteed basic standard of living, and the elevation of workers' dignity above the pursuit of profit.'
The Jewish Chronicle

Blue Labour

For Catherine, Harry, Thomas, Anna and Isaac.
Without whom . . .

Blue Labour

The Politics of the Common Good

Maurice Glasman

polity

The right of Maurice Glasman to be identified as Author of this Work has been asserted in accordance with the UK Copyright, Designs and Patents Act 1988.

First published in 2022 by Polity Press
This paperback edition first published in 2024 by Polity Press

Polity Press
65 Bridge Street
Cambridge CB2 1UR, UK

Polity Press
111 River Street
Hoboken, NJ 07030, USA

ISBN-13: 978-1-5095-2886-8
ISBN-13: 978-1-5095-2887-5 (pb)

A catalogue record for this book is available from the British Library.

Library of Congress Control Number: 2022930010

Typeset in 11 on 14pt Sabon
by Cheshire Typesetting Ltd, Cuddington, Cheshire
Printed and bound in Great Britain by CPI Group (UK) Ltd, Croydon

The publisher has used its best endeavours to ensure that the URLs for external websites referred to in this book are correct and active at the time of going to press. However, the publisher has no responsibility for the websites and can make no guarantee that a site will remain live or that the content is or will remain appropriate.

Every effort has been made to trace all copyright holders, but if any have been overlooked the publisher will be pleased to include any necessary credits in any subsequent reprint or edition.

For further information on Polity, visit our website:
politybooks.com

Contents

Acknowledgements   vi

Introduction   1

1 What's Going On?   11

2 The Meaning of Socialism   32

3 From Contract to Covenant   62

4 Democratic Renewal   95

5 Internationalism versus Globalization   120

Notes   144
Index   152

v

Acknowledgements

This short book has taken a long time to write.

Blue Labour has always been a relational politics and sometimes it is hard to know how to clarify honestly where responsibility lies. I can only say that I put the book together in my own way.

Within Blue Labour, I wish to acknowledge the conversation and contribution of Cheryl Barrott, Luke Bretherton, John Clarke, Jon Cruddas, Ruth Davies, Rowenna Davis, Bernard Donoughue, Paul Embery, Ian Gearey, Jack Hutchison, Adrian Pabst, Jonathan Rutherford and Richard Tuck. I am grateful for their friendship. The Sunday evening group of Kat, Paul, Debs, Dave and Sam have helped me in more ways than I can say.

The Common Good Foundation has supported my work over several years and I thank Judy Hopkinson, Tobias Phibbs and Bryn Phillips for their daily support and encouragement. Leslie Deighton, Mark Dembowski, Jamie Lindsey, Gavin Long, Jenny Sinclair and Phillip Ullman have all contributed to this book in important ways. Arnie Graf and Jonathan Lange have

Acknowledgements

been resolute in their friendship throughout the years and taught me the truths of organizing. Father John Armitage kept reminding me to read Catholic social thought. Andy Haldane has been a constant partner in working through the political economy and I appreciate his friendship greatly.

George Owers, my editor at Polity, has displayed all the virtues: patience, courage, generosity and faith. His assistance is much appreciated.

Above all I am overwhelmed with love and gratitude to my wife Catherine and my children Harry, Thomas, Anna and Isaac.

I have dedicated this book to them.

Introduction

Blue Labour was born during the financial crash of 2008 and the dismal twilight of New Labour and the Third Way. It was also the time of my mother's death. She had a terrible condition called progressive supranuclear palsy and I saw her become a mute witness to her own degeneration. The two came together in Blue Labour as I tried to make sense of the loss both of my Mum and of Labour. The uncritical embrace of globalization, the domination of finance capital, combined with a pitiless progressive modernism, left no place for workers in the movement they had created. It was a case study in alienation. My Mum left school at 13 to work in a factory so she could support her four younger sisters and her ill father, who died a few months before I was born. My love for Labour came from her. She told me how they built the National Health Service, how Hackney Council moved her family from a damp basement to a council flat, led the fight against Hitler and shared her fanatical commitment to 'education'.

As she lost her capacity for speech, all I could do was watch television with her. We stared together at the unfolding financial meltdown as the combined assets of many generations were lost in speculative hubris. We watched Gordon Brown saying that it was the 'destiny of labour to save the global banking system' and my Mum's eyes met mine and then she shook her head and closed her eyes.

That was when Blue Labour was born, and it turned out to be a river with many currents running through it. Some of them are philosophical and find their source in Aristotle and what is now called virtue ethics, taking in Aquinas and Alasdair MacIntyre along the way. Some are Christian, ranging from the dissenting tradition based on association, liberty and conscience, through that of Catholic social thought and its critique of capitalism based upon the dignity of labour, local democracy, solidarity and the stewardship of nature. These in turn were rooted within a biblical tradition which first articulated that human beings and nature are sacred and not simply resources for the accumulation of power or money. While Blue Labour expanded and the conversations intensified, there was a shared recognition that all these things were embodied in the Labour tradition itself and their recovery was essential for its renewal.

It became clear that any politics that could draw inspiration from the Pilgrimage of Grace and the Putney Debates, from Archbishop Laud and Gerrard Winstanley, from Saul Alinsky and Ernest Bevin, was not going to find its home within a movement dominated by Whiggish assumptions. The roots of Labour lay in its covenantal bond with the British working class. The culture and experience of workers shaped the form of the Labour movement. It was of them, by them and for them, and that was no longer the case. The steady disaffection of the working class from their party was the source of its 'progressive palsy'.

'Blue' Labour began as a recognition of the sadness and demoralization that had beset the party movement and tradition by 2008. It was compromised, lacking in vitality and severed from the roots of its renewal, relationally and conceptually. Things don't only get better, and the lack of understanding of loss and tragedy required a rearticulation of the fundamental tenets of the Labour tradition and the belief that these are both relevant and true.

The first truth is that human beings are not commodities, but creative and social beings longing for connection and meaning. The second is that nature is not a commodity either, but a condition of life and a sacred inheritance. The Labour tradition also asserted that democracy is the best way to resist the domination of the rich and the educated and that the leadership and participation of the working class is central to this. Further, it argued that local democracy is vital, as well as forms of economic democracy that can hold state and market powers to account; a democracy that is both locational and vocational.

More than that, Labour drew upon historical memory, and not only rational argument. It drew upon the Norman Yoke and the tradition of the freeborn for the solidarity required by its associations. It demanded not only a human status for labour but also a move from the contractual to the covenantal. The human status of labour required the binding of capital to reciprocal obligations, the strengthening and not the abolition of inherited institutions such as Parliament and the common law. Labour was rooted in class but was a national party, and its internationalism was rooted in democratic nation states, in which sovereignty was required in order to domesticate capital.

Within the Labour tradition, the liberties were held to be sacrosanct, and there were four fundamental forms: freedom of religion, in which no-one could be coerced in their faith, and that meant freedom of religious practice; freedom of conscience, in that no-one could be coerced in their beliefs; freedom of expression, in that people were free to speak and create and to reject and criticize; and freedom of association, which was the fundamental form of the trade union movement, which was banned for a century before it was accepted. Within Labour, liberty and democracy are not opposed but mutually supportive political practices.

Blue Labour was also born of a recognition that any vital political tradition and movement has to go beyond rational philosophy and embrace paradox, to combine seemingly contradictory elements in new forms. Labour is a paradoxical tradition, far richer than its present form of economic utilitarianism and legal progressivism. The Labour tradition is not best understood as the living embodiment of the liberal/communitarian debate, or as a variant of the European Marxist/social democratic tension. It is robustly national and international, conservative and reforming, Christian and secular, republican and monarchical, democratic and elitist, radical and traditional, and it is most transformative and effective when it defies the status quo in the name of ancient as well as modern values. The Labour tradition has a vast and varied assortment of traditions, stories and accomplishments, great and small, and can tell a story of how things could get better out of the materials inherited from the past. And yet the technocratic managerialism of its dominant ideology could not draw upon its history for its renewal. Its radicalism, nourished by its roots, was displaced by policy driven by its head, and it was very unattractive.

This type of political tradition is to be distinguished from matters of philosophy. Philosophical arguments, like policy proposals, aspire to be universal, coherent and reasonable. Such demands may be useful in the final stages of a policy review when specific recommendations have to be ordered, but remain unsuited to either political action or ethics. Historical continuity, democracy, the necessity of extemporized action and the demands of leadership render politics contingent, comparative and paradoxical in form. Ideas are not ultimate and singular in politics, but contested and related. The English nation, above all, is deeply synthetic in form, constituted by different tribes and people who generated an unprecedented form of common law, common language and an inheritance of a commonwealth. Its political parties and movements have been stubbornly synthetic too, a matter of blending folk and academic concerns through a politics of interests. Political movements which are rooted in the lives and experiences of people bring together new constellations of existing political matter. What to philosophers is an incoherence can be a source of vitality and strength to a political tradition which contests with others for democratic power over its vision of the common good.

Two ancient political traditions came together in the Labour movement. One could almost call them ancestors. On one side was the Aristotelian notion of the Good Life and the Common Good. In this the importance of politics, of virtue understood as a pursuit of a common life between estranged interests, was carried into the political life of the nation. The founders of the Labour movement understood the logic of capitalism as based upon the maximization of returns on investment and the threat this posed to their lives, livelihoods and environment, but they did not embrace class war and clung stubbornly to an idea of a common life with their rulers and exploiters and the democratic renewal of their inherited institutions. The Labour idea of the person, in which the plural institutions of civic life have a vital effect on the flourishing of the individual and are inseparable from it, is explicitly Aristotelian. This is an important root of the conservatism in the Labour tradition, a concern with the preservation of status, limits on the market, an attachment to place, starting with the common sense of people (*doxa*) rather than with external values and a strong commitment to a common life. This is also a direct link to the self-consciously Aristotelian Tudor statecraft tradition of the sixteenth century, which engaged with the balance of interests within the realm, pioneering endowments to promote the sciences and commerce, developing apprenticeships and slowing enclosures. The 'Commonwealthmen' movement in the early twentieth century, of which G.D.H. Cole and R.H. Tawney were active participants, are part of that tradition.[1]

The second ancestral tradition within which Labour was embedded is that which followed the Norman Conquest and actively pursued the idea of the balance of power within the Ancient Constitution and the 'rights of freeborn Englishmen'. It was on the basis of the violation of customary practice that people resisted the subsequent enclosures and assertion of

Royal Prerogative in the name of Parliament and championed the liberties threatened by the domination of one institution alone. Labour takes its place within a far longer national tradition of resistance that values a legal and a democratic order, that is both reforming and traditional, in simultaneous motion. Parliamentary socialism, the National Commonwealth, whichever way Labour chose to describe itself in its first fifty years, acknowledged its attachment to the language and sensibility of the politics of the commonwealth and a central role for the inherited institutions of governance that represented the interests of what used to be known as 'the commons', the House of Commons not being the least of those. The early theorists of Labour economics had a commitment to natural law in which there were prescribed limits as to how a person could be treated by political authority, and by economic ones, too. In England, in particular, these natural laws were assumed to have existed in this country before the Conquest, so they were not abstract, but embedded in the political history of the nation. Democracy and common law were used as ways to constrain the domination of the monarchy. Parliament was vital in this, as was the Church. This sensibility found Labour form in the work of Robert Blatchford and William Morris and the 'guild socialism' of G.D.H. Cole, S.J. Hobson and A.J. Penty.

It is far too rarely acknowledged that, alone in Europe, Labour succeeded in generating a workers' movement that was not divided between Catholic and Protestant, or between secularists and believers; instead the movement itself provided the common life within which these potentially antagonistic forces could combine in pursuit of a common good. In cities like Glasgow and Liverpool, as well as London and Birmingham, this was an extraordinary achievement. This is perhaps the most distinctive feature of the Labour tradition, as opposed to social democracy in Europe, which was far more explicitly secularist in form. The non-established churches, for reasons of historical self-interest, were committed to freedom of association and expression. The churches that nurtured the Labour movement were associational forms of religious solidarity, severed from state power and concerned with preserving a status for the person that was not defined by money or power alone. Aristotelianism flowed predominantly through the Catholic Church, the rights of freeborn Englishmen through the Protestant congregations of the South and the Midlands, and they came together in the Labour movement, which was committed to religious freedom. It was, indeed, a broad church.

The London Dock Strike of 1899 is a classic expression of the Labour movement in action, built on the assumption that only organized people could resist exploitation, and the forging of an alliance between Irish and local workers, brokered by the Catholic Church and the Salvation Army. The local Labour Representation Committees were the new institutions within which the previously unrelated forces met and within which leaders were elected, strategy was discussed and actions were planned. It is here that the 'labour aristocracy' of skilled workers who had lost their status and small-holders who had lost their land make their appearance, drawing upon customary practice as a means of defying managerial prerogative. The courage of the strikers was remarkable. To disrupt trade was viewed as unpatriotic and seditious as the British Empire was a maritime emporium with London at its hub, and the force of the navy and army as well as the police was threatened against the strikers. The laws of the maritime economy, freely contractual, was held to apply to the port, which was excluded from territorial legislation.[2] To build a successful political coalition on the basis of stable employment and wages was a great founding achievement of Labour politics. With Cardinal Manning, accompanied by William Booth and the Salvation Army Band, leading the striking dockers on their march, it was very difficult for the employers to use force and depict them as an undisciplined rabble.

The sheer ferocity of the market storm within which Labour was born in the nineteenth century, the scale of the dispossession – of property, status and assets – generated by the creation of the first ever free market in labour and land, the simultaneous enclosure of the common lands, the criminalization of association, the scrapping of apprenticeships and the eviction and proletarianization of the peasantry meant that the only port in the storm was the security that people found in each other.

The burial given by the Co-operative Society is another example of the retrieval of status generated by the Labour movement, the dignity of death given by solidarity in life. The pauper's grave was one of the most fearful fates of dispossession. It was a combination of subs-paying membership, co-operation with chapels and churches and the practices of mutuality and reciprocity that provided the resources out of which a human status for the person could be retrieved and retained. The reverence for life, the honour given to each member through his or her membership and dues, were not drawn from a secular or modernist ethic, but a radical solution that was fashioned from traditional assumptions and practices. Labour as a radical tradition was crafted by both workers' and Christian institutions as they confronted the hostility of both an exclusivist state and an avaricious market. They called their ideology socialism and their party Labour.

The fourteen years since the birth of Blue Labour have not been happy ones. Labour has lost four elections in a row, losing increasing levels of working-class support. Ernest Hemingway observed that people go bankrupt in two ways, gradually and then suddenly. The same could be said for Labour's divorce from the people of its heartlands, which has in turn enabled the Conservative Party to form a new class coalition, consummated by Brexit.

The Party is weak but the tradition is strong. It offers a framework within which previous mistakes can be rectified, and a plausible claim to rational superiority to its rivals. The Labour tradition, alone in our country, resisted the domination of the poor by the rich, asserted the necessity of the liberties of expression, religion and association, and made strong claims for democratic authority to defy the status quo. It did this within a democratic politics of the common good that resisted violence and strengthened democracy.

The argument of this book is that it might be a good idea to do it again.

1

What's Going On?

The era of globalization was based upon the idea of change without continuity, of a modernity without tradition. The consequences were deemed inevitable and alternatives were considered nostalgic, populist or doomed. As technology knew no borders, as stable employment evaporated into transferable skills, enormous changes were embraced as necessary. Immigration was viewed as a fate outside of political negotiation, universities were expanded, house prices surged, manufacturing was replaced by the knowledge economy, real physical presence was replaced by virtual reality, the relationships and constraints of community were replaced by self-defined identity. Choice was elevated as the ultimate freedom even as it was entirely constrained by technology, markets and law.

And yet this view of reality wasn't true.

Traditions were subdued but not eviscerated; the realities of an embedded and embodied life upon the earth were lived and shared between people. Love endured through the disenchantment, and democracy was not entirely subordinated to procedure. Those who benefited most from the new arrangements, the rich and the educated, articulated their interests in terms of universal values and historical inevitability. The values were those of aspiration, mobility and openness, in opposition to the unpleasant interests of place and work, and any resistance was characterized as reactionary and futile. The captivation of Labour by what might be called 'capitalist modernity' meant that it could not articulate or pursue resistance to its acceleration. The categories of labour, land and money were rendered beyond political contestation, and each was defined as a commodity.

Underpinning this was the idea of revolution, that the era we were entering into was unprecedentedly different. This was foolish in two ways. The first is that there is always a continuity through time; that the very idea of revolution is a defiance of, and blinds people to, the persistence of matter and memory. The second is that it renders the experiences of the past inaccessible and impermissible. Thus Tsarist imperialism could not be linked to Soviet policy, nor Napoleon to the French kings.

And Labour took a revolutionary approach to itself. The Labour movement was a curious thing, its leadership and membership taking the form of a broad-based Christian movement, a distinctive blend of Catholic, Methodist and dissenting with a dose of High Church Anglicanism. The Christian concepts of love, brotherhood, the dignity of labour, of community and solidarity, and even the Kingdom of God that sometimes peeked through, formed the fundamental language of the movement. While the Social Democratic Federation and the Fabians were resolutely secular, this was not the case for the workers' movement. The Christian inheritance of labour is a treasure of renewal; its critique of capitalism, fired by the dark satanic mills and their wicked indifference to suffering, is a constitutive aspect of its inheritance but is rendered inaccessible if a revolutionary secularism prevails. The ecumenical tradition of the Labour movement, often described as a 'broad church', indicates that Labour was a cross-class coalition as well, combining a radical liberalism with a more communitarian ethos, middle and working class, countryside and city.

In the pantheon of the Roman Gods, Apollo and Mercury represent two different types of people and peoples. Apollo was rooted in place and represented stability and honour, agriculture and war. Mercury, in contrast, was swift and mobile with a delight in trickery, music and literature. They were both quick to see each other's vices. For Apollonians, Mercurians were cunning, lacking in courage, while valuing money and success over reliability and faithfulness. Likewise, the Mercurians considered the Apollonians slow, stupid and provincial. Both groups have co-existed in society since ancient times, Apollonians dominating the countryside and Mercurians flourishing in the cities.[1]

In the development of the British polity, this tension, between the Court and the Country, the city and the countryside, London and the provinces, became characteristic of its politics and both forms of life, the settled and the transient, the durable and the fleeting, the productive and the commercial, the crafts and the arts: they all needed each other. The tension between them constituted the distinctive character of the polity, characterized by a comparatively extreme form of tradition and modernity, conservatism and radicalism, continuity and change. The pioneer of industrialization and the home of finance capital also preserved the monarchy, Parliament, common law and the established Church.

Politics was in large part a negotiation between these groups. The Mercurians offered ever-expanding horizons and wealth on their terms; the Apollonians were wary of the offer, fearing the loss and insecurity this would bring. The relationship between progress and dispossession and the rate of change were publicly negotiated. A settlement would come unstuck if the balance of power tilted too much towards the Mercurians, although the direction of travel was clear. The Tories, in the nineteenth century, became the dominant political formation by adopting the clothes of the Apollonians while implementing the policies of Mercurians.

What is distinctive about the past forty years, the era of liberal globalization, is not only that it claims that all virtues are held by Mercury, that the battle is to be won by the swift, the mobile and the qualified, but also that it breaks any notion of mutual dependency with the Apollonians, and this disdain has come to be reciprocated. The latter became, to quote the only line of poetry from Hillary Clinton's 2016 campaign, a 'basket of deplorables'; the places in which they lived, reservations for the losers and the 'left behind', those unable to change and embrace the possibilities opened up by an increasingly Mercurial world. Tony Blair expressed this view when he described the character of the global, liberal economic order in a speech in 2005.

> The character of this changing world is indifferent to tradition. Unforgiving of frailty. No respecter of past reputations. It has no custom and practice. It is replete

with opportunities, but they only go to those swift to adapt, slow to complain, open, willing and able to change.[2]

This assumption concerning the direction and speed of change is what made the Brexit vote, and then the distant, subterranean thud of the Trump explosion, so disconcerting. The echoes of further disruptions in Poland, Brazil, India and Hungary were heard not as expressions of a theoretical or political weakness that needs to be corrected but as manifestations of stupidity and nastiness, verging on the psychotic, within the people who vote that way. A tradition, socialism, that pioneered a sociological understanding retreated to a moralistic psychology that renders the world inexplicable. The 'wrong side of history' was exacting its revenge on Mercurian hubris.

It is still of significance. The Conservative victory of December 2019 was based on a new class coalition, with the ex-industrial working class abandoning Labour. It indicated a profound disaffection with a Mercurian agenda.

This revenge is overturning the fundamental assumptions of political rationality that have organized our politics for the last forty years. A trend towards globalization, multiculturalism, secularism and human rights is resisted by democracy, nationalism, religion and particularity.

For many on the left, the world has gone mad and bad. The left is virtually unrepresented in Central and Eastern Europe; it has disintegrated in its citadels of France and Belgium. In Britain, the Labour Party's embrace of the ideology of globalization has rendered it isolated and estranged from its roots. It no longer embodies the hope of working people. As an organization, it is not even in a relationship with them.

Perhaps the best way to understand it is that Britain is going through an interregnum, a time 'in between times' when the consensus that previously united parties and underpinned policy is being publicly contested. Such a period is an argument over sanity, over the limits and meaning of what it is reasonable to believe and do. The economic power of China and the internet platforms intensifies: the era of globalization persists, and there is no constructive alternative to replace it.

Antonio Gramsci described an interregnum as a time 'when the old is dead and the new cannot be born ... when there is a fraternization of opposites and all manner of morbid symptoms pertain'.[3]

The new takes on a monstrous form in which we are besieged by 'populists' and 'authoritarians' who offer democracy as a form of resistance to a globalized economic order that has no place for any form of power that protects the interests and values of the working class. In such a period, the new is perceived as mad, bad and dangerous, an unreasonable spectre from the past that indicates a dystopian future. It is threatening and destabilizing to the self as well as the polity. The intensification of the prescribing of opiates and other forms of legal anti-depressants and painkillers has become one of the central features of this interregnum.[4] It is a time of betrayal, confusion, anxiety and moral panic. The market storm is accompanied by political turmoil and the questioning of the most fundamental institutions of political order.

For four decades, a dominant political consensus has

supported opening up national societies to markets and then integrating them into increasingly global markets. Globalization promoted the corporation over the nation state and the market over democracy. The redistributive capacity of the nation state was diminished and the political realm of democratic nations was weakened.[5] Economic policy making became increasingly detached from politics. Society was treated as if it were an abstract space. In the words of Pierre Manent, it was occupied by 'the unlimited rights of individual particularity'.[6] It ceased to be organized by institutions, characterized by a distinct language with its own culture, and became instead a random collection of individuals located in a particular place. What G.K. Chesterton called the 'democracy of the dead', a sense of continuity with the past, was besieged.[7]

The modern political system is defined by a double commitment: to democracy, on the one side, and a global financial system, on the other. The conflict between political self-government and global capitalism is the principal tension. The balance between them is one definition of politics within which the claims of capital to commodify human beings and nature have been resisted by democracy. The settlement following the Second World War, for example, was brokered as a response to this tension, which unleashed its demons in the 1930s. In that settlement, a distinction was made between free trade in real commodities, those that were produced for sale in the market, on the one side, and human beings, nature and money, which were not, on the other. This distinction was discarded in the 1980s and this was institutionalized in the form of the European Union (EU) via the Maastricht and Lisbon Treaties. The abandonment of democracy and the embrace of the market felt like the breaking of a covenant.

The distinctive feature of globalization over the past forty years is that it sought to overturn the assumptions of the post-war settlement by subordinating democracy to treaty law, agreed between states but outside of the control of parliaments to amend.[8] Free trade is conflated with free movement and this then leads to the formation of a market society, which disintegrates, as its only bonds are self-interest and contract. This might be called the liquidation of solidarity. As people are social beings with a natural tendency to attachment and relationship, they turn to sources of solidarity that are inherited and, in that sense, arbitrary in order to associate to gain some respite from the market storm. If globalization is a rational order, then democracy and community are considered unreasonable.

In order to understand this, it is necessary to analyse the component parts of the ideology of globalization. Globalization consists of the four powerful forces of (a) capitalism, (b) member statism, in which obligation is to elites in other countries rather than the population of your country, and (c) liberalism within the framework of (d) a technological determinism that renders borders irrelevant. Each is based upon the unmediated movement of people and commodities through space in which the fundamental units are the abstract individual outside of history and relationships, and a collective based upon a constitutional legal order underwritten and constrained by multi-national treaties. Globalization eliminates the possibility of politics to challenge this order, but maintains the state structure to enforce it.

Capitalism treats human beings and nature as commodities: fungible objects to be moved about, exploited and discarded on the basis of the maximum return on investment. Its distinctive feature is that the very substance of society is turned into a market, with fluctuating prices setting the value of human beings, land and food. This is what we refer to as a market society. It is unsustainable as the organizing principle of society, leading to human and ecological degradation, powerlessness and inequality.

A member state is one in which intermediate institutions are subordinated to centralized control in the name of procedural justice. It is mistaken to assume that capitalism works alone: it is, in all cases, in partnership with a Leviathan, or state, which creates the conditions of the enforcement of a contractual society. Member statism is a form of domination in which political sovereignty loses its democratic nature and takes on a primarily administrative form.[9] As the state defined politics as a technocratic redistribution of resources, rather than a mutual space of negotiation for the creation of a common good, there is little reciprocity or accountability in this model. Without a democratic society to hold it in check and challenge its centralizing authority, it can and has become a form of domination that undermines liberty and pluralism.

Liberalism in its market, identity and utilitarian forms has been the dominant ideology that has shaped both market and state in recent decades. Liberalism is a theory that views the individual as formed outside of relationships and attachment and which conceives of emancipation as breaking the mutual bonds of constraint. It tends to subordinate democracy to the economic, technical and legal realms and political conflicts are reduced to managerial, technical or economic tasks. In this, capital is allowed to treat society itself as a domain of the economy. A system of market-based practices is imposed on the public as well as the private sector. It assumes the narrow self-interest of each one of us as an autonomous chooser. While there is a constant exhortation towards society, big, networked or civil, it continues to disintegrate.

In contrast, the argument developed here is that a common life is capable of being negotiated and that is the essence of politics. For example, immigration is a political issue which was hived off into the legal and constitutional order. Free movement is not an incontestable right and legal rights are always a political achievement. They require consent from a political community. They can be lost and their maintenance requires strong democratic support. This basic truth has been lost during the period of liberal ascendency when legitimate political concerns about immigration and regional or industrial policy are often considered illegal.

In a globalized world order based upon capitalism, the administrative state and a liberal constitution, a sense of a belonging, of place, of work, of mutuality and responsibility is undermined through a lack of power. The point of democratic politics is to shape and preserve a home in the world against the threats of domination and dispossession and to maintain the structure of society in the face of intense forces of disintegration. This points to the fundamental role of community organizing. These forces isolate people and disempower them from acting democratically to shape a human response, so that any reaction that is essential to democracy is dismissed as populist.[10]

The point of this book is to articulate a politics in which democracy and liberty are mutually supportive rather than hostile forces. In order to renew itself as a national political force, Labour needs to break its commitment to globalization, in which its domestic agenda is subordinate to its international commitments. The Brexit impasse was a symptom and not a cause of the present interregnum, and through Labour's inability to distinguish between internationalism and globalization it appears as a force that maintains a bankrupt settlement.[11] It does not think creatively about the democratic renewal of inherited political and civic institutions such as the City of London or City and Guilds but seeks their abolition. Institutional diversity is subordinated to procedural uniformity. Labour cannot offer respite from the demands of an unconstrained global order and the precarious powerlessness it generates.

For Labour, the obdurate persistence of the working class haunts its politics like an ancestral ghost. It was assumed the past was dead but it is alive and the progressive condition of historical amnesia was principally generated by the emergence of New Labour and the response of social democracy to the ascendency of the New Right and the collapse of Bolshevism. The superficiality of the Third Way analysis had profound consequences, and in order to win the war of position in this new interregnum it is essential to understand why that analysis was plausible and then why it was wrong.

How We Got Here

The interregnum of the 1970s was resolved by the election of Margaret Thatcher and then Ronald Reagan. This was not so much a change of governments as a different regime based upon its critique of the limits of the post-war settlement. The New Right cast the history of post-war Europe into a narrative. The fundamental problems of the post-war settlement were defined as bureaucratic domination, institutionalized trade union power, the interference of non-economic factors in the functioning of market systems and the increasing growth of the state.[12] This led to stagnation, inflation and government confusion combined with the repressive use of state power; all processes occurring simultaneously.

The New Right defined itself against the prevailing consensus, which it argued could not address or understand these problems, let alone solve them. The New Right went on the ideological offensive in order to remove capitalism from political contestation, to subordinate the democratic power that can be used to resist its domination and to strengthen the domestic and global police force to enforce the new order. It could do this because it was able to understand the problems confronting the prevailing institutional arrangements in a newly intelligible way. This opened up the space for an explanation of why people should reject the existing settlement and embrace the practical and theoretical superiority of the New Right's prescriptions for preserving freedom and renewing society. It argued that state interference perverted just allocation while encouraging paternalism and, in Eastern Europe, tyranny. The cause of 'stagflation' was the arbitrary interference of the state in a complex economic system it could not predict or control. Detailed central direction of economic and social life was unworkable as well as immoral. This line of thinking was subsequently developed by right accelerationists who argued that any attempt to interfere with the price system and technology was doomed to failure, repression and poverty.[13]

The New Right defined the crisis of the 1970s in political, economic and social terms. The political crisis was one of 'governability'. The demands made upon the state were escalating, leading to overload and confusion and a subsequent dissolution of public order. Michel Crozier, Samuel Huntington and Joji Watanuki summed this up well in their report to the Trilateral Commission when they wrote: 'While it has been traditionally believed that the power of the state depended on the number of decisions it could take, the more decisions a modern state has to handle, the more helpless it becomes.'[14]

In the economy, excessive taxation was penalizing risk and innovation. The welfare state distorted labour supply and eroded managerial authority. Privatization was seen as essential to unburden government, free up markets and impose managerial discipline. State planning was a methodological delusion in global markets. The sovereignty of the consumer lowered the tax burden on the citizen. The fundamental change was that labour was subordinated to capital. The marginalization of trade unions was central.

Economic stagnation was explained through renewed categories of classical economics. Three truths were assumed. The first was that markets consist of individual agents who exchange goods and, if left to their own devices, achieve an equilibrium between demand and supply through the medium of prices. The second was that the economic sphere is autonomous and should not be disturbed by society or government. The third was that agents act to maximize their advantage.

The post-war settlement was defined as an extensive system of racketeering in the form of price and wage fixing in labour, property and money markets. There were too many political interferences in the system that were the result of previous political settlements. History interfered with a well-ordered economy, and in the economic sphere history was abolished and a new market storm was inaugurated. The New Right succeeded in enforcing its conception of global order, and the system it established remains – despite platitudes about civil society and social capital – the institutional and ideological framework within which the politics of the EU operates.

As Margaret Thatcher told Ronald Butt of the *Sunday Times*, the aim was to end the collectivist society of the post-war years. Economics would be the method, but 'the object' she said, 'is to change the soul'.[15] Its ultimate victory was to change Labour's soul.

By 1991, the sociologist Anthony Giddens was describing British society as experiencing an acceleration of modernity. Everyday life was continually being transformed. The new capitalist modernization was creating what Giddens called a post-traditional order. Greater degrees of personal self-expression were weakening class ties. An identity politics of gender, race and sexuality was displacing the politics of class solidarity.[16] The German sociologist Ulrich Beck described the changing relationship of the individual to society as 'individualization'. A new kind of 'capitalism without class' was freeing individuals from the constraints of the old order.[17]

Philip Gould, one of the main architects of New Labour, found inspiration in the 1992 Clinton presidential campaign. He wrote in *The Unfinished Revolution*, 'In the twenty-first century the pace of change will be so fast, so all-embracing, that it will in effect be an age of permanent revolution.'[18] All the fallacies of Marxism were being uncritically appropriated in terms of revolution, technological determinism and the progressive direction of history while all its insights into the political economy, alienation and the power of capital were being disregarded.

In the United States, Bill Clinton and the New Democrats developed a progressive politics that combined socially liberal values with economic liberalism. In the late nineteenth century, and again in the 1920s, progressive politics had stood for a resistance to oligarchs and banking monopolies, safe workplaces and a strong commitment to education. Increasingly it adopted a Whig theory of history which believed that history progresses through individual rights and global markets. In doing so, it became ever more legal and technical, with a strong stress on supranational and codified constitutional forms that would constrain democracy. In this modern guise, it became the theoretical basis of globalization.

Under the Third Way regime, associated with Bill Clinton in the United States, Tony Blair in Britain and Gerhard Schroeder in Germany, capitalism was liberated from national government and national democracy. Robert Reich, Clinton's Secretary of Labor, described what he called progressive globalization. 'There will be no national products or technologies, no national corporations, no national industries. There will no longer be national economies'.[19] In this period, capital, understood as the combination of technology, finance and knowledge, was exported, mainly to China, which did establish a national economic system and an industrial strategy.[20] The nation state remained a crucial driver of the economy and yet it was discarded. This was the most profound change.

Britain's liberal market transformation and the decimation of a national economic system provided fresh impetus for the integration and identity of the EU as it emerged from the European Economic Community, known in Britain as the Common Market. The 1986 Single European Act had created a European Union with a single market, 'in which the free movement of goods, peoples, services, and capital is assured'. Barriers to trade, including public contracts, state aid, financial regulation and 'discriminating standards', would be steadily dismantled to create a single undifferentiated market. The Maastricht Treaty in February 1992 formally tied the single market to Economic and Monetary Union. Free movement superseded free trade.

In June 2000, the Lisbon summit committed Europe to a new strategic goal of becoming 'the most competitive and dynamic knowledge-based economy in the world'. Its priorities were a more urgent approach to economic competitiveness and the creation of a new European worker 'capable of taking charge of his or her employment destiny'. These were policy goals echoed in Labour's 2001 White Paper on *Enterprise, Skills and Innovation*, which called for education and training to create workers who would be autonomous entrepreneurs rather than dependent employees.

What's Going On?

In 2004, ten more countries, eight from the old Eastern bloc, joined the EU. The Labour government, unlike other EU countries, decided against transitional controls. It calculated that levels of immigration from these countries would be negligible. They weren't. Between 1997 and 2010, net immigration quadrupled, boosting the UK's population by more than 2 million. New Labour's politics of deregulated employment markets and the free movement of labour was the undoing of progressive politics. It set the political conditions for the vote to leave the EU in 2016. It had radically disturbed the balance between Apollonians and Mercurians and there was little politics could do to respond.

This new liberal political settlement enacted by Thatcher and consecrated by Blair produced a trans-national consensus and a trans-partisan political elite. Conservatives had adopted liberal economics. They controlled the sphere of the economy. The liberal left controlled culture. Its class power lay in its role as the arbiter of cultural taste and the interpreter of national interests, and in its control of the institutions of media, learning and culture.

Globalization had promoted the corporation over the nation state and the market over democracy. There was a governing consensus about opening up national markets and integrating them into increasingly global markets. The redistributive capacity of the nation state was diminished and the political realm of democratic nations was weakened. In 2005, the share of national income going to wage earners, after a brief rise, had begun to fall again. Household debt had risen as cheap credit replaced depleted welfare provision.

Life was becoming precarious for a growing number of people, graduate and non-graduate. Giddens' post-traditional society had suggested liberation from the shackles of the past. In fact it was unpicking the ties that bound people into association with one another. The pressure on Labour to accommodate to globalization led to the abandonment of its covenantal commitment to the labour interest and the cultivation of solidarity required for society to function. And Beck's individualization was proliferating and dispersing the sites of class injustice and inequality and making solidarity much harder to achieve. It brought with it the costs of loneliness, mental illness and a loss of meaning in life. New Labour's embrace of globalization led to a growing sense of disenchantment amongst its working-class support.

Labour's electoral success had been partly dependent on the extraordinary longevity of the economic boom. The 2008 financial crisis brought it to an end. The banks were rescued from collapse by an unprecedented bail-out with the largest transfer of assets from the many to the few since the Norman Conquest. The Governor of the Bank of England, Mervyn King, put it well when he said that 'never in the field of human endeavour had so few owed so much to so many'.[21] The taxpayer was saddled with the debt and the subsequent austerity. Meanwhile the bankers continued to reward themselves as they saw fit.

What did Labour stand for? There was no obvious answer. It had allowed capitalism to treat society as a domain of the economy. Its economic policy was increasingly detached from democratic politics. Political problems were treated as economic, technocratic and legal policy issues. In England, there was no redistribution of power to localities that was not managerial and fiscal. There had been no development of the appropriate relationship between state, market and society, and of the role that the Labour movement and a Labour government could play in generating a good life for the people of the country. Class conflict had been neutralized by administrative fiat and economic-technical thinking.

By 2010, thirteen years of unprecedented electoral success, sustained redistribution, the building of a more open society, the renewal of public buildings and improvements in public services had nonetheless left Labour with an identity crisis. In the General Election, the Party, now led by Gordon Brown, suffered its second worst defeat since 1931.

Labour lacked a political, economic and social analysis of its own failures and found itself committed to the form of global economic order that it had actively constructed but which was the biggest constraint on its renewal. The Ancient Constitution found itself subordinated to a legal and economic order that upheld the priority of Treaty Law over national democracy. And that Treaty Law made it illegal to resist capitalism. Under the leadership of Ed Miliband, there was no attempt to reconcile the commitments Labour had to globalization and the type of national agenda that could redress the concentration of assets and power through a renewal of the national economy, or address working-class exclusion from its benefits. Labour had no vision of a democratic politics that could articulate a politics of the common good.

Jeremy Corbyn could. Coming from a Bennite tradition that upheld parliamentary sovereignty, accountability and a strong analysis of the problems with the pre-vailing global political economy, he could speak to the renewal of Labour's soul and its role in brokering a new settlement. As the Brexit referendum loomed, he could have led the arguments for leaving the constraints of the Maastricht and Lisbon Treaties behind and articulating the importance of internationalism and the active support of people who are being oppressed and exploited all over the world. He could have articulated a European Federation bound by peace and free trade but not bound by political union and the forms of enforced economic uniformity that remove capitalism from political interference. He almost did this in the election of 2017. The nationalization of water and the railways; the rights of workers to have the first attempt at buying their own companies in case of sale; an industrial strategy that included the endowment of regional banks: all of these generated energy and support. The commitment to respect the result of the referendum also resonated with previously estranged working-class Labour supporters.

Almost – but not quite. Labour lost the Brexit interregnum and its ability to build a broad-based coalition to resist the domination of capital and extend democracy, to preserve the human status of labour and respect for nature. It retreated to an accommodation with globalization and lost the Labour heartlands. The class basis of the Party had shifted to the Mercurians.

The Labour movement and Labour politics has a vital role in the restoration of a democratic politics and restoring the primacy of society. The politics of the movement must return to the politics of the common good, seek to build and endow institutions that uphold value and belonging, restore the integrity of place, the dignity of labour and the virtue of solidarity. Only by drawing upon its precious but neglected traditions can Labour articulate a plausible vision of the future. It must move from a contractual to a covenantal politics defined by a commitment to the human status of the person, the renewal of inherited liberties and institutions and a sustained resistance to the domination that debt and commodification bring.

2

The Meaning of Socialism

Human Beings, Belonging and Relationships

Blue Labour is formed from many traditions and brings them together in a distinctive synthesis. It draws upon Aristotelian ethics in relation to virtue as good-doing rather than do-gooding and begins its politics within the experience and values of the community rather than imposing an external good from outside. Democracy is decisive in that politics. It draws upon the covenantal tradition in relation to debt, the dignity of the worker, land reform and mutual obligation as first developed in the Bible, and more specifically elaborated through Catholic social thought and its critique of capitalism. With equal intensity, we draw upon the tradition of the Labour movement and its specific practices of association, organizing and building the 'strength of the weak' in defiance of capitalism and the administrative state, both of which can undermine liberty and democracy.

The Labour movement itself drew upon ancient traditions of the Norman Yoke, of the freeborn English, in order to develop its politics of democracy, liberty and accountability. It was a paradoxical politics in which the Kantian promise of treating people as ends in themselves, of equally distributed freedom as reciprocal liberty, takes its place beside Edmund Burke in terms of the importance of tradition, institutions and a sense of attachment. A meaningful politics brings together many forms of ethical and historical matter into contingent alignment, and part of their energy is found in the tensions and contradictions, historically, intellectually and in terms of coalitions. This is one of the reasons why political philosophy is so bad at either explaining or guiding politics. In its search for coherence, it confronts a reality it cannot comprehend.

People are social beings, and socialism, as a tradition of interpretation and action, assumes that we are partially constituted by an inheritance of language, relationships, place and belief. We are not simply rational heads making choices but also embodied beings, living in a world we didn't choose, born to parents we didn't choose, speaking a language we didn't choose in a place we didn't choose.

An important part of our flourishing is to ensure that the institutions we inherit are good and that we pass them on to the next generation. Life is not only about choice but also about obligation, stories as well as statistics, relationships as well as ambition. The recognition of the different traditions out of which people fashion an identity is central to our politics and they are the ethical constituents out of which we generate meaning. Politics is creative; there is no singular static community that serves as our ground. As social beings, we assume that a sense of belonging to something larger than ourselves is constitutive of who we are. The political conclusion is that in order for an individual to flourish, we require a flourishing society. This is in contrast to a conception of the person as a liquid node moving through undifferentiated space.

As meaning-seeking beings with a tendency to attachment and relationships, we have the ability to use language to both negotiate with others and imagine different realities. We are, as Aristotle argued, '*zoon politikon*', political beings, in that we can negotiate a common life with others, and, through democracy, evaluate our common decisions and revise them. We are neither communitarian beings, with a singular identity defined by one community, nor liberal autonomists, outside of all relationships and inheritance. Democratic politics is about how we live together with others under conditions of civic peace with shared institutions on terms of non-domination. Labour politics is how we do so through a shared acceptance of mutual dependence mediated by democracy, while maintaining a political sovereignty that can challenge the domination of capital, in terms of money and technological power, and a commitment to the four liberties of association, religion, conscience and expression.

Communities, Pluralism and Difference

Blue Labour's politics is defined by pluralism and organized by the pursuit of the common good. It is an agonistic politics in that conflict and difference will always be present and decisions are provisionally settled in a temporally revisable way through democracy. An election is not the will of the people; it is simply a national political decision that is legitimate until the next election. The only rule is that you have to do it again. Democracy is an important part of our civic inheritance and it needs to be deepened in the economy and the locality.

The different groups and classes that constitute society have interests that require negotiation and an exploration of the possibility that there is a commonality between them. Sometimes conflict takes the form of class, sometimes of religious or ethnic communities; sometimes small towns are dominated by big cities and there needs to be a recognition of the threat of domination and a political culture that can negotiate a mutual interest and develop the institutions required for a common life. This requires that narrow self-interest is transformed into a self-interest broadly conceived, so that there can be a mutual interest in a common good. That is the task of our politics, which Bernard Crick describes as 'ethics done in public'.[1] It is argumentative, angry and divisive, particularly when the fundamental consensus of the polity is disputed and its resolution requires the building of relationships within and between communities.

One of the reasons politics is fraught and ugly is that it matters. Democratic decision has force and losing is always a possibility. This does not affect your legal status as a free and equal citizen, but it does affect your power and it defies your own conception of the good. There is, however, no alternative to politics, and democratic defeat requires reflection and a reformulation of both political position and strategy drawing upon neglected aspects of a political tradition in order to deepen and broaden alliances. That is what is required of the Labour tradition now, as the Owl of Minerva flies.

Blue Labour does not privilege one particular community or identity over others. We tend to the tragic over the progressive and do not believe that there is one class blessed by history, or that history unfolds towards human perfection. There is no singular community that is the custodian of the common good or the embodiment of progress, although we take particular inspiration from the Labour tradition itself. It is simply untrue that 'things can only get better' or that the arc of history bends towards justice. Blue Labour promotes the reality of pluralism, locality and shared institutions as a starting point of political association. It values the parochial because it is about the task of learning the social virtues that govern our everyday lives and which, taken together, constitute what Aristotle conceived as shared assumptions concerning the good.

Understanding and working within this common sense is necessary in order to participate in a political conversation in which assumptions can be questioned. Belonging to a political community is necessary in order to bring about change within it. Everything cannot be put in doubt simultaneously, because if it is, no stable reference point of common conversation can be maintained.[2] A shared language ensures that this is the case. Blue Labour has always sought a broad-based coalition between different communities on issues of mutual concern, such as the living wage or limits on interest rates. This is also the reason for Blue Labour's respect for faith communities: they preserve a sense of the sacred in relation to the status both of human beings and of nature which is vital to a politics that can resist commodification. It is a politics of non-domination and of negotiation and seeks to broaden the base of political participation. Our starting point is political economy.[3]

The preservation of society through democratic association was the practice of the Labour movement. It required a common good between estranged communities, which at its origin were Catholic and Protestant workers, and a cultural move away from polarization and towards the building of a shared life through the expansion of the commons in defiance of private claims to the exclusive ownership of land, knowledge and technology.

The fundamental ethos of Labour is the practice of democracy as a way of life that governs association between free people. This is so with regard to the state in terms of electing representatives to Parliament as the sovereign body which makes laws. Parliament works within the interpretative frame of the common law and is sovereign, in that it can enforce its laws. Labour, as a force in British politics, embraced this institutional tradition because it could make changes within it through democracy. It was not prevented from establishing a National Health Service, for example, by a written constitution. There was no institutional impediment to changing the law if Labour could gain democratic support in Parliament. It allied itself with the existing institutions in order to establish labour as a constitutive aspect of the nation and to represent a labour interest that had been ignored by, or was invisible to, both conservative and liberal traditions. As important is that the forms of the Labour movement itself were democratic.

Labour was not a revolutionary movement. Labour developed its own form of Burkean socialism in which a desire to represent its class 'in and for itself' was combined with a robust attachment to the renewal and democratization of the inherited institutions of government. It was also committed to local or municipal democracy and it was in the cities that Labour formed itself as a governing force; through a social democracy characterized by mutual institutions such as the building and burial societies that were created and owned by their members.[4] This tradition of mutuality was constitutive of the Labour movement and is central to Blue Labour. It is only by the representation of working-class interests in politics, the economy and society that some constraint on capital and its tendency to dominate, and then to commodify, can be fashioned.[5]

The Common Good

The common good is about recognizing that there are differences in our society and these are intensifying. Differences of interests and beliefs between capital and labour; religious and secular; immigrant and local; men and women. There are inequalities of power as well as wealth, and those with an inheritance and assets will dominate those without.

The common good is a politics that holds that people are capable of negotiating a common life; that a person is not a commodity to be exploited and then discarded but a human being capable of love and creativity, as well as selfishness and greed. People may tend towards the good but are also capable of bad. The path we take is not to be found in our human nature – there are too many examples of both to be satisfied with any theory that says we are definitively one or the other. Rather, it is found in what society respects and rewards and what it punishes and condemns, whether there are incentives to vice or incentives to virtue.

A good society promotes and strengthens justice, civic peace and mutual sacrifice and recognizes the truth that we share a common fate. Pertinent here is Jeremiah's injunction to 'seek the peace of the city . . . for in its peace you will find peace'.[6] There is a mutual interest in the common good which is based on the mutual flourishing of all in which each person contributes to society and benefits from belonging to it and participates in its institutions, both civic and political. Democratic politics is the way we create practices and institutions that enable people to live with each other with a mutual regard. We are all in exile and need to find a way of living together and of bringing different traditions and stories into relation with one another in order to fashion a common life based on solidarity and reciprocity.

For Labour, the bads of the economy are the starting point for this kind of politics. It begins with resistance to commodification.

That is the point about human nature. It is futile to ask whether we are egoistic or altruistic: we are both and neither at different times and in different circumstances. The assumption made here is that we have a mutual interest in being able to care for our loved ones and pursue the practices that are meaningful to us: the security of our homes, resisting corruption and having the capacity to lead a good life with others. Constraining the dominance of the market is central to this. It must also recognize that the art of association, of a democratic life, is one that is learnt through the experience of participating in shared institutions.

The politics of the common good takes a paradoxical form by assuming that tension and conflict are necessary for a common life; that pluralism is the basis of solidarity; that inheritance shapes the future; that tradition is necessary for modernity; that co-operation is necessary for competition: in short, that the old is part of the new.

The politics of the common good is a tradition of negotiation between estranged interests that has its roots in Machiavelli's *Discourses* and in Catholic social thought. Both traditions of thought, Christian and Republican, stress the capacity of human beings for self-regard and domination, what both refer to as the 'incentives to vice' that exist within structures of power and wealth. Both argue for 'incentives to virtue' that provide reasons for people to be less conspicuously self-interested and promote the goods of honesty, mutuality and non-domination. It is impossible to comprehend the motivational structure of capitalism without having some conception of vice, sin or domination and the need for accountability.

Democracy and the Nation

Blue Labour is built on the assumption that being good is difficult and that there are powerful interests that reward greed and dishonesty. Capitalism rewards selfishness and avarice; politics rewards instrumentalism and evasion. There are good reasons, however, for arguing that a good life is based on constraining those desires and promoting democracy, mutuality and respect for others with whom we need to build a common life and to assert that we are vulnerable, dependent beings. Death, desertion and dereliction are realities and it is right that a politics should uphold a good based upon the understanding of mutual dependence and ensure that it does not become one of domination, through strengthening democracy rather than retreating into an exclusively rights-based politics. Central to this is a public life that is itself a form of accountability. It is also through politics that people can find meaning and hope. Sadness is not a pathological condition but a sober response to prevailing realities. Democratic politics should offer solidarity and connection and the promise of meaningful change, an alternative to a powerless, enraged isolation or a communitarian revenge. Although it should be kept to a minimum, politics is part of life and cannot be avoided. We recognize that technocratic liberalism pursues a vision of fulfilment outside of all relationships and limits that subordinates politics. This needs to be challenged.

Democratic politics is the principal means through which people have resisted the drive to the commodification of human beings, their institutions and nature. Labour politics is precisely that: a coalition of people working together to preserve their humanity and inheritance. It requires institutions with power that can constrain the market. Labour was founded as a politics of working-class agency, through which workers could achieve recognition and participate in the polity as a power. It was not, however, in its original form exclusively statist. It sought to strengthen the social, and to extend democracy within it. It developed the institutional ecology of a counter-culture built upon democracy and mutuality, upon sharing the burdens and benefits of association through accountability and participation: a politics of earning and belonging.

41

In order for Labour to renew itself, it is necessary to build a broad-based coalition that is committed to the common good, or the mutual flourishing of the component parts of society. This requires the renewal of the body politic: the cities, counties and other civic institutions through which people participate in self-government. It is necessary to work with the affections of the people in order to generate a democratic politics that can shape external threats and dangers into something comprehensible and to develop new institutions, revive old ones and pursue policies that can hold the power of money and management accountable. The disintegration of society, of the social, is the result of the domination of markets and states, the logic of which undermines durable forms of local and vocational association.

The Labour tradition has deep roots in British history, and they are tangled, rooted in different interests and periods. It is the inheritor of many traditions, ancient and modern. What is required is a politics that challenges the rationalism of contract through a revival of the idea of a covenant, of a promise redeemed that is as strong for liberty as for democracy. It is a covenant that binds different generations into a story rooted in the renewal of a shared inheritance based upon democracy and liberty, and the understanding of our national, civic and natural ecology as a shared inheritance.

The role of government is to facilitate the growth of the decentralized institutions needed to generate a common good between estranged communities and open the space within which a better life can be pursued. To do so requires recognizing the permanent threat of domination by the few of the many, most particularly under conditions of extreme market penetration and the pincer movement on society by both state and market. Care for parents and children has become financialized.

Blue Labour argues that the democratic nation state and the common law remain the best means of safeguarding the rights and freedoms of people. Neither the abstract ideal of the individual nor appeals to humanity offer a political community capable of guaranteeing a democratic order and the rights and protection of citizens. That is the inheritance that Labour helped secure and should be faithful to.

There is a distinction between internationalism and globalization and that distinction is profound. Globalization is a system that promotes the unmediated movement of people, money, goods and services through space. It is based upon four assumptions, the first of which is that capitalism is the best system of economic organization and should be protected from political and societal interference in the name of efficiency and superior outcome. The second assumption is that the state should be essentially procedural. The third assumption is that the best system of international co-operation is based upon constitutional liberalism in which the rights of the individual and of property are given priority. Finally, the fourth assumption is a form of technological determinism in which borders are no longer of relevance in the economic and communicative sphere. Internationalism, in contrast, is an active form of solidarity with those who are being exploited and oppressed. Blue Labour is internationalist in its orientation.[7]

Aristotle and Karl Polanyi; commodification and societal resistance

Blue Labour challenges the liberal capitalist order but it does not belong to the revolutionary left. It places itself in the tradition inherited from the international and national labour movements and the democratic practices and ideas they grew out of, as well as Christianity, in its intense variety, and most particularly Catholic social thought. Our politics begins in ordinary everyday life; in our labour, which makes the things we need, and in our life as social beings in relationships and families, together with the places we live in. These are the activities that Aristotle speaks of when he describes the end of political association being 'life and the good life'. In order to preserve these things, it is necessary to be radical and recognize the threat posed to a settled life by incentives to vice in the economy and polity.

The importance of Aristotle to our politics is three-fold. First, he locates the starting point of politics as lying within the *demos*, as located in the assumptions and experience of citizens and not externally in rationality alone. Second, he understands the good in terms of a practice, a learnt virtue which gives a central role to institutions in upholding non-pecuniary goods. This is linked to the subordination of individual rationality to reason, which, Aristotle argued, emerged from public deliberation between free and equal citizens. The third concerns the voraciousness of human desires, the consumer lust that a money-based economy generates and the risk of immediate self-gratification undermining the virtues and sacrifices necessary to generate a common life with other citizens.[8] Aristotle argued that money led to extremes of wealth, gluttony and cowardice and that citizenship, friendship and familial obligation were not commercial relationships. Politics was the public practice through which the common institutions of self-government preserved the sense of community necessary to subordinate money. Democratic politics remains the fundamental practice through which the domination of money is resisted, and the Labour tradition provides the best comparative framework for pursuing that.[9]

Karl Polanyi's anthropology and theory of history, developed in *The Great Transformation*, builds this argument around three propositions.[10] The first is continuous with Aristotle and argues that people are sociable and relational beings. The second point relates to the distinction between dependence and domination. Aristotle argues that we are all dependent on a physical environment and other people for the satisfaction of needs and our existence. The fundamental question is how to organize that dependence so it does not become domination. The third proposition is that the economy requires social institutions that preserve the status of human beings and nature as something other than commodities. Commodities are defined as objects produced for sale on the open market and subject to fluctuating prices. Commodification takes place when something that was not produced for sale, such as human beings and nature, becomes available only through market exchange.[11] The fundamental process of capital is to turn all aspects of society into commodities.[12]

Societal institutions protect the cultural resources of society from depletion and exhaustion by constraining the market and educating the person in the internal goods of a practice rather than external goods such

45

as money, power and fame.[13] Polanyi argues that the market economy is based on three 'commodity fictions', labour, land and money, none of which are produced for sale and which are, therefore, not commodities at all. In a market society, however, these become 'factor markets' when, in reality, human beings and their natural environment are the 'substance of society'.[14]

Labour, Polanyi argues, is not a commodity, as people are not produced for sale. It is also inseparable from the body and life of a person.[15] The second commodity fiction of land is 'only another word for nature'. Even free market economists cannot claim to have created the world.[16] The third commodity fiction of money is produced by the state as a token of exchange and not as a saleable commodity.[17]

The theory of history developed by Polanyi is that as society develops in size, technological capacity and complexity, it tends to be eliminated by the centralized state, on the one hand, and the competitive market, on the other. The emerging nation state subordinates the existing civic institutions such as cities, guilds, corporations, churches, parishes and municipalities by the imposition of unmediated sovereignty within its borders. The market, in its turn, opens up the substance of society for sale in the open market. The self-generating link between individualism and statism is driven by their mutual contempt for societal institutions and traditions. Those autonomous social institutions which organize the satisfaction of needs and the preservation of a practical culture are considered a constraint on the individual freedoms of the person and the political will of the state. Squeezed between the individual maximizer and the collective aggregator, society, understood as a self-governing network of institutions, disintegrates.

Polanyi claims that the idea of the economy as a self-regulating system of exchange grounded in individual choice, governed by prices and constrained by scarcity is based on an impoverished conception of the importance of the economy and its institutions in the reproduction of ethics and society. He calls the extension of the market into all forms of society 'market utopianism'.[18] This conception of economics seals off the economy from any kind of societal or democratic interference in the name of choice and efficiency while expanding its domain to include all elements of culture as conforming with the motivation of rational self-interest. The market becomes a self-fulfilling fallacy as the power of the state is used to define all conceptions of rationality and agency which do not conform to the principle of interest maximization as populist, irrational and ultimately illegal.[19] The imposition of market society always involves violence and the centralization of power: 'The road to the free market was opened and kept open by an enormous increase in continuous centrally organized and controlled interventionism ... it required a conscious and often violent intervention on the part of government which imposed the market organization on society.'[20]

States and markets are thus mutually necessary at the initial stage of a nation's formation as regards uniformity of taxes, tariffs and the free movement of labour and capital within its sovereign territory. States and markets are also self-generating in that the breaking of society, its patterns of work and local modes of association, its culture, leads to the emergence of two dominating systems: the market as the principle of dynamism and the state as the representative of generalized, or abstract, community. Unmediated dependence on the market for a fluctuating wage leads to unmediated dependence on the state for relief as the state takes on a welfare role. The political rationality of nationalism is that it could resist the pressure of capitalism through the institutions of the state, but in doing so it subordinated the plurality of societal institutions still further. It is the eradication of the reciprocity embodied in autonomous and decentralized societal institutions that leads to the domination of market and states and the liquidation of society.

The tension between the commodity fictions and the substance of society is the central dynamic in Polanyi's theory and derives from two meanings of economic: the formal and the substantive.[21] The formal refers to the rational calculation of means and ends under conditions of scarcity, the activity of economizing, defined as the greatest frugality of expenditure in the securing of ends. The substantive definition of the economy concerns the material satisfaction of needs. The 'economistic fallacy' is the conflation of a formal process of calculation with the substantive practices of production. The imposition of a formal model on society eliminates ethics from the economy, institutions from the organization of production and any motivation other than self-interest from the domain of rationality. This has a deleterious effect on the capacity of individuals in society to co-operate in the reciprocal satisfaction of wants and needs.

For Polanyi, there are periods of intense change, which he describes as 'market storms', in which the substance of society is imperilled. He gives three examples: enclosures, industrialization and the collapse of the gold standard in the inter-war years. His stress is on the rate of change and the ways in which the resistance of society and the adoption of a new form of statecraft allow society to reconstitute itself.

An example of this is the Tudor and early Stuart policy of using the power of the crown to slow down the societal disintegration caused by enclosures. Polanyi argues that the monarchy and the Church defended the 'human and natural substance of society' from the effects of the privatization of the common lands, which were 'wasting its towns, decimating its population, turning its overburdened soil into dust, harassing its people and turning them from decent husbandmen into a mob of beggars and thieves'.[22] The principal means of doing this was through the Poor Law of 1601 and the Statute of Artificers of 1563. The latter required seven-year apprenticeships, yearly wage assessments and national enforcements of labour statutes.[23] England became the first country in Europe to enforce a national vocational system. It extended guild organization into armaments and luxury goods and, from a relatively backward position in all areas except the production of tin and pewter, by the seventeenth century English cannons were in demand throughout the continent and a competitive advantage was established in silk, glass and the manufacture of fine paper.[24] Through resisting enclosures, enforcing vocational labour market entry as well as establishing grammar schools and expanding universities, the 'fabric' of society was rewoven without being rent. The Tudor state endowed local institutions which upheld the status of labour, extended and defined a national educational system and embedded these in a local civic ecology. They established a form of statecraft that strengthened the body politic and that allowed for the development of democracy within its structures.

Two centuries later, the menace of industrialization was far more severe. The failure of the basic income model of Speenhamland led to the emergence of a utilitarian political economy in which both the commons and the poor law were abolished and 'nature's penalty' of hunger was considered the most effective incentive. While Thomas Hobbes argued in *Leviathan* (1651) that men behaved like beasts, Joseph Townsend argued in *A Dissertation on the Poor Laws* (1786) that similes were superfluous. The causes of poverty could only be overcome by the imposition of a new incentive structure. The Poor Law Amendment Act of 1834 established the first free market in labour. Wage subsidies and outdoor relief were abolished. The Bank Act of 1834 subordinated the domestic economy to the gold standard and the Anti-Corn-Law Bill of the same year established a free market in food. A market society replaced a market economy. Human beings and nature became commodities dependent on wages and rent, their survival dependent on money. They had no status.

John Clare expressed a common sentiment when he wrote:

> Inclosure came and trampled on the grave
> Of Labour's rights and left the poor a slave
> And memory's pride ere want to wealth did bow
> Is both the shadow and the substance now.[25]

Or as Polanyi writes: 'An avalanche of social dislocation, surpassing by far that of the enclosure period, came down upon England.'[26] He argues that while '[l]aissez-Faire was enforced by the state, resistance was spontaneous'.[27]

There was a resistance to commodification which clustered around land, labour and knowledge. The distinction between the formal and substantive economy provides Polanyi with his theory of historical agency. During the last third of the nineteenth century, society succeeded in disentangling real commodities from fictitious ones.[28] Many forces in society were part of the double movement and it did not necessarily assume a progressive form. In some societies, the peasantry, Church and aristocracy went into alliance, and in Britain, the Labour movement played an important role. In all cases, society was protected from the market through resisting commodification. Politics constrained markets.

Polanyi describes this response as the 'double movement' of society in response to industrialization. On the one hand, economic liberalism reduced human labour to a commodity. On the other hand, the extension of the market into society created a counter-movement of working people who sought to conserve society and defend their human status in defiance of the free market and the poor law state. They drew upon a range of beliefs to do this: inherited stories, civic institutions and ideologies ranging from the freeborn English, the Norman Yoke, Christianity, in almost all its forms, through to socialism and conservatism. There was an explosion of working-class self-education initiatives, not least the Workers' Educational Association.[29] What they all shared was that people's lives had a status and dignity that was irreducible to their cash value alone and that it was necessary to associate together in order to resist their dehumanized state. Custom, tradition and memory proved vital in developing a politics that could resist the domination of capital.

These are enduring themes. The shadow of the Norman Conquest remained as an example of an attempt to impose personal rule without consent or accountability involving the seizure of land and the imposition of a foreign language.[30]

This counter-movement organized the labour interest in popular organizations of mutual self-help. The labour interest resulted from two events. The first was the exclusion of the working classes from the political life of the country in the 1832 Parliamentary Reform Act. This led to the 'Ten-Hour movement' to limit the working day and to the struggle for factory reform. The second event was the 1834 Poor Law Reform Act, which established a competitive market in labour and turned people's labour power into a commodity by abolishing the Apprenticeship Laws. In different alliances and in different ways, an educational system was established, housing was built, the ten-hour day was introduced, the vote was extended and the commons was re-established through public parks in urban spaces. Freedom of association led to the emergence of trade unions, insurance mutuals and friendly societies, local government and public sanitation projects. The flourishing of associations, from football clubs to professions, became a central feature of nineteenth-century life as society was reconstituted from exclusively local to national associations of mutual interest.

The third market storm was the inter-war years and the rise of Fascism. Polanyi argues that: 'The stabilization of the currency became the focal point in the political thoughts of people and governments; the restoration of the gold standard became the supreme aim of all organized effort in the economic field.'[31] In a monetized economy, the value of a currency becomes a vital determinant in the satisfaction of needs. The protection of the currency became the prime responsibility of the state and led to the subordination of politics to the demands of fiscal orthodoxy. The irony of national sovereignty, particularly in central and eastern Europe, was that its attainment led directly to financial subordination within the international economic system. Any measures taken by the state to relieve unemployment and societal strains were punished by currency collapse and capital flight. In Austria in 1932, Belgium and France in 1926, Germany and Britain in 1931, social democratic governments had to resign from office for the sake of a stable currency.

The reasons Polanyi gives for the emergence of Fascism are that through the pursuit of a stable currency, states were debarred from intervening in the economy so as to alleviate suffering or prevent societal disintegration. 'Questions of social organization had to be wholly subordinated to the need for the restoration of currency.'[32] Any form of resistance to the idea of a society only governed by prices and contract was defined as impractical, immoral and populist. The role of politics was subordinated to markets, even as the scope and power of states grew.[33] The tendency towards passivity and isolation was visible to contemporaries. Max Weber, in his essay on the failed revolution in Russia in 1905, wrote:

> The question is this: how are freedom and democracy in the long run at all possible under the domination of highly developed capitalism? Freedom and democracy are only possible where the resolute will of a nation not to allow itself to be ruled like sheep is permanently alive.[34]

The priority of fiscal policy undermined both democratic parties and statecraft. Polanyi's explanation is that once economic rationality becomes severed from the institutions necessary for the reproduction of the substance of society, there will be a violent reaction embodied in a communitarian state as reciprocity has broken down. Against these two notions of a disembedded rationality and a disembodied polity, he proposes the idea of a substantive society.

Socialism, in this definition, is the defence of the social, of society, sustained by non-financial relationships of trust and mutual concern bound by shared institutions. The form of governance is democratic, the practices those of association and reciprocity. Polanyi is not making an argument for the elimination of markets in real commodities or against an active role for the state in the governance of the economy. He insists, however, that a substantive society requires an economy based upon non-market institutions which play a role in the provision of needs, the distribution of knowledge and the allocation of status. There are three spheres in which reciprocity, exchange and redistribution are each the dominant practice. Exchange describes uncoerced transactions between parties resulting in the reappropriation of title and is characteristic of a market exchange. This is based on contract. Redistribution pertains to the state and designates a transfer of goods to the centre and their subsequent reallocation. Reciprocity is the principle of society and refers to give and take through time and the strengthening of a mutual interest. Reciprocity is the basic principle of society.

The Labour tradition has always asserted the meaning of labour as the practice through which society reproduces itself and creates the conditions of free self-government. Labour has two meanings: childbirth and toil. Together they form the reproductive substance of society. As well as seeking meaning through relationships and attachment, we find meaning through our work. Within this, capital, as the most dynamic force of dispossession and debt, is resisted by the idea of 'labour' as a source of value and community which is not an arbitrary inheritance but is actively constructed by co-operative human effort and based on relationships and association. Thus, association and trust remain alive in society and retrieved from the endless churn.

Nostalgia is the insult most frequently aimed at those who draw upon memory, culture, institutions and tradition in order to resist the domination of capitalism and renew democracy as a practice of self-government. Nostalgia is a translation of the Greek word for a longing for home: *nostos* means homecoming. It is all the more threatened by the knowledge that a home is not an eternal birthright, or rooted in an uncontested homeland, but a contingent and provisional achievement. Every settlement is a negotiated settlement. A home in the world is a political achievement. It is based on accepting neither capitalist modernity nor communitarian menace but a negotiation of a common life based on reciprocity, association, liberty and democracy rooted in a politics of relationship. Historical inspiration is not by its nature fatuous and false. There is a great deal to admire in the early Labour movement and it remains an exemplary tradition.

Such a politics is not only about change and modernization but also about resistance, and democracy as a means of refusing a form of modernity defined by money markets and administrative states which together eliminate society and the possibility of a home. In this view, nostalgia, the longing for a home, is a force for resisting dispossession and retaining forms of a common life. Parliamentary sovereignty is the condition of this because it asserts a countervailing power to that of markets alone. A sense of loss and a desire for restoration is shared between many communities and can find expression through the renewal of the Labour tradition and the institutions of democratic self-government that it initiated.

Blue Labour is not a communitarian politics because community is not a static, unitary inheritance. We are constituted by a plurality of communities – religious, cultural, locational and vocational – and we actively shape and reform our inheritance, in our own lives and in the polity. A sense of solidarity requires shared institutions and experiences in which sacrifice for the common good is freely given. Freedom in society is one way of conceptualizing this; socialism is another.

The present task of the political imagination is to grasp the possibilities of the democratic renewal of society, to move towards a genuine 'social democracy'. Labour remains the primary political tradition for resisting the rule by the rich of the poor. That resistance needs to be rooted within the lives, culture and experience of working-class people who have been excluded over the past forty years. The key resources for this lie within the Labour tradition itself.

In the political realm, sovereignty is necessary in a democratic nation. It is the source of the agency that constitutes a polity. For Blue Labour, this 'we' is a political community that is made up of different identities and interests that can be brought together in a participatory and representative democratic politics of the common good. It draws upon people's political and ethical traditions and negotiates a common commitment between them. This covenant upholds the liberty and mutual obligation of all citizens and subjects, places limits on debt, protects the integrity of nature and defends the institutions that uphold justice, knowledge and mutuality.

Sovereignty is not simply about people 'taking back control' of their lives. It is about re-establishing the necessary source in time and place of the agency of our political institutions.

A democratic self-governing society built upon the participation of its citizens in the exercise of power and its accountability is the fundamental goal of the Labour movement. There are good reasons why the peculiar combination of institutions that combine liberty with democracy, modernity with tradition, that are summarized by the idea of the Ancient Constitution, and the goal of extending this into the economy, are worthy of retrieval and celebration as a constitutive part of Labour's inheritance. This is based on the balance of interests rather than the separation of powers – in other words, on politics.

The fundamental issue revolves around the idea of an inheritance and whether it should be abolished or democratized. The question is whether socialism is a complete rupture with what went before or a transformation of an inheritance that enables people to build a home together on the basis of reciprocity, participation and democracy. Blue Labour is not revolutionary, it is covenantal.

The task is to articulate a renewed statecraft that disrupts the dynamics of globalization and financialization through building democratic civic institutions, and which is led by the renewal of the Labour movement as a power rooted in place and the economy. This means moving beyond an exclusively urban coalition and actively building political support in the small towns and countryside, which feel excluded from our politics. In Britain, we tend not to refer to our nation but to our country, and that is the starting point of democratic renewal: a retrieval of geographical, institutional and historical diversity and turning that into a national system that protects human beings from commodification. That is what the four forces that make up globalization wish to eliminate. The renewal of democracy depends on building a resistance to that, one which is based on the preservation of the distinctive and particular sources of affection and loyalty that persist despite the homogenizing swirl of globalization.

Conclusion: Labour's Struggle

Labour's traditions originate in the philosophical debates that shaped English modernity and in the popular resistance to the liberal market system of capitalism found in local as well as religious traditions. It stood for the virtues necessary for the exercise of democracy and liberty. It was bound not by the pursuit of narrow individual self-interest but by the common good. In its scepticism towards grand theoretical design, its rejection of political violence and its popular attachment to ancient English liberties, it was a product of national tradition and the inheritance of the Ancient Constitution as much as a response to the global imperatives of capitalism and the international labour movement.

Labour embodied the social ethic and stood for modernity and tradition. It was catholic and dissenting, radical and conservative, and it combined these traits in a distinctive form that could build a transformative coalition and a popular democratic politics.

While Labour is continuous with various long-standing traditions within the British polity, its distinctiveness came from understanding the particularity of capitalism and the power of money in modern society and the threat this posed to the human status of the person and his or her ability to live a meaningful life.

During the market storm of the 1980s, the market economy expanded and tried to impose a market society as the profit motive seeped into every aspect of relationships and public life. Private wealth plundered public assets in a storm of privatization and contracting out. Central to this were the twin processes of concentration and commodification. The tendency of capital is to concentrate ownership. The free market leads to monopoly, or, if regulated, to oligopoly. We see this tendency in internet companies where what was supposed to be a free market of start-ups has now emerged as Facebook, Google, Amazon, Apple and Netflix. The tech utopia led to the age of the oligarchs.

Blue Labour is founded on the idea that human beings are not commodities and on a new kind of political economy rooted in Labour history and practices. The goal is the development of a decentralized national economic system that resists the tendency towards the centralization and concentration of assets and wealth.

This would be a system that gives incentives to democratic participation and in which the governance of the economy becomes part of the common life.

Labour was established to represent the labour interest; it was of the people, by the people and for the people. Its original demands were the extension of the franchise, the eight-hour day, affordable housing and freedom of association. In order to retrieve that position, the economy needs to be embedded within societal oversight and direction. The preservation of society through democracy was the practice of the Labour movement. That requires a reconciliation between estranged communities and a cultural move away from polarization and towards the building of a shared life through the expansion of the commons in defiance of corporate monopoly of land, knowledge and technology.

This is the heart of the issue of the meaning of socialism, which has always been torn between the desire to retrieve a home from the churn and dispossession of capitalism and the embrace of a dehumanized modernity in which family, place and work are unwanted remnants of a pre-modern culture that generates 'false consciousness' and turns workers away from revolutionary politics. This is Marx's point when he writes in the 'Eighteenth Brumaire' that we don't make politics under circumstances of our choosing but that the 'tradition of all dead generations weighs like a nightmare on the brains of the living'.[35] The early Labour movement working with the inherited materials of the commonwealth havered between the land reform advocated by the Chartists with their rejection of free trade and an embrace of industrialization and a reform of the existing system.

What was resolved upon was to restore society as a non-commodified space of relationships rooted in liberty and organized around democratic associations. The freedom to discuss heretical and dissident ideas was seized and people came together to debate, build their organizations and stand in elections. It became the most significant political force of its time because the common good politics it developed was built by working-class people reclaiming their home in the world. For Labour, that was the meaning of socialism.

Central to this was the understanding of the *Rerum Novarum*, these new things that constituted capitalism. The renewal of Labour's political economy is of fundamental importance to its political renewal.

3

From Contract to Covenant

The economy is the means by which society satisfies its needs and wants through combined effort. In complex societies, this always involves an intense combination of individual, state and societal engagement. The economy we inherit works in the interests of capital, of those who own or manage the inheritance of previous generations, understood as ownership of technology, property and money. This has intensified over the past forty years at the expense of labour.

Capital, in its essential form, is promiscuous. It seeks the highest possible rate of return at the fastest possible speed. Once the returns begin to slow, it seeks new partners that can deliver higher returns more quickly. When there are no constraints on the relationships it can initiate, and end, and when capital is the fundamental organizing principle of the economy, the consequence for society is ruinous.

For a century, the response of the left has been to advocate a role for the state as the exclusive principle of economic organization, and this has led in each case to the eventual surrender to the market. The weakness is that there is no price system that can communicate what people want and a centralized administrative system inhibits innovation. The Soviet Union disintegrated following a period of market reforms; China became the driver of globalization by creating the conditions for sustained production and the importation of capital as the central principle of production, with no recognition of the human status of labour.[1] The first principle of New Labour was the acceptance of globalization and the diminishment of labour value and power. The task now is to conceive of a role for the state in preserving the human status of labour and the vulnerable status of nature through an institutional system that facilitates the renewal of society.

The promise of Labour, and of socialism more generally, was to domesticate the destructive power of capital, the commodification of human beings and nature. It did this by strengthening democracy as an alternative mode of power to that of capital, within a framework that upheld the fundamental liberties of religion, association, expression and conscience.

Labour reneged on that promise.

What is required is a form of political economy that can domesticate the destructive tendencies of capitalism by moving from contract to covenant as the central principle of economic organization. This requires the return of state power and the engagement of different interests in the governance of the economy.

The idea of a covenant is important because it addresses the fundamental problems of the economy; the inequality generated by debt; and a system of debt forgiveness that strengthens mutual obligation. It includes nature as a partner and has a role for institutions in brokering a common good across time and space. It indicates a way that place, work, solidarity and nature can be bound into an economic system. In other words, it domesticates the demonic energy of capital by binding it into relationship with the very forces it seeks to commodify.

Contract, in contrast, is an isolated event, an exchange of equivalents between hands that by definition is indifferent to external consequences, long-term trends or context. A contract is a legal agreement between two parties which has led, over time, to the domination by the rich of the poor, the concentration of assets in fewer hands, the dehumanization of labour as a human factor, the exploitation of the environment and the neglect of relationships and place. The idea of covenant is sometimes treated as a biblical curiosity with no relevance, yet it is central to political authority, in that Parliament and common law are inter-generational forms of authority. In specifying limits to levels of debt, the inherent status of the human being as requiring work and shelter, a partnership with the land as a common good and the strengthening of community within the economy itself through the binding of estranged interests in a shared endeavour, it provides the institutional means of building a decentralized national economy.

In short, covenant requires that human beings and nature are not treated as commodities, and that there is an inter-generational commitment to the common good between classes and regions based on the renewal of place. This gives shape to the change of consensus that is required to remedy the defects of what went before. Neither the state nor the market is sufficient to generate a good society: it requires the renewal of society, and its representation within the economy in the form of vocational and locational institutions that negotiate a common good in changing circumstances, by upholding the status of labour, land and knowledge as part of a shared inheritance. Covenant is a means of turning domination into a conscious form of mutual dependence by constraining both the market and the state through the strengthening of society.

Changing the Consensus

Any political consensus defines what people can achieve through democratic co-operation and what has to be left to the co-ordination of the price system. Over the past forty years, redistribution, regulation, tax revenue and interest rates have been considered to be appropriate central state functions within the economy. A market system based on fluctuating prices, in parallel, has been considered the most efficient means of communicating what people want. Beginning with the dominance of the New Right in the 1980s, the state was not considered a rational agent within the economy and as a result its function became exclusively external and regulatory.

This missed two fundamental truths. The first is that the economy is an eternal form of all societies as the common activity through which the satisfaction of material needs and wants can be achieved by the transformation of nature into goods through the exertions of labour and the application of skill. It is a substantive need rather than a formal model.

Labour is a necessity in both of its meanings. It is the means through which society reproduces itself through biological and cultural reproduction. Each person is dependent upon a physical environment and other people for the satisfaction of needs. This in turn requires institutions that preserve and renew knowledge as a means of reproducing the necessities of life. This intensifies in a complex society. Work has a necessity and a history that is not grasped by understanding labour as an exclusively utility-maximizing activity carried out entirely by the individual agent. This is why human capital is a limited concept, in that it does not show adequate regard for the institutional inheritance that makes skilful labour possible. When it comes to labour, we all need an inheritance.

This is linked to a deeper fiction, propagated by economic theory and outlined in the previous chapter on Karl Polanyi, which is that human beings and nature are treated as commodities – defined as objects produced for sale on the open market – to be exploited efficiently by competitive markets in labour, land and food. This is because the imperative within capitalism is to turn human beings and nature into commodities when they were not produced for sale in the market and are irreplaceable. What economists call factor markets are just another description of the substance of society, human beings and nature, which is another term for creation itself.

The problem with the breakdown of political economy into a system of maximization of returns within the economy and then a redistributory and regulatory state as a means of mitigating the hazards and providing collective necessities in the form of money payments and administrative services is that it does not engage with the problem at source. It then enforces the fiction, thereby generating a more powerful need for a state to protect the basic conditions of life. The innovation in the recent cycle is that the banks and corporations receive state protection. What Andrew Haldane defines as the 'doom loop' – the nationalization of risk and the privatization of gain – is unsustainable as a principle of economic governance.[2]

Virtue, Craft and Reciprocity: Blue Labour Economics

Blue Labour economics assumes that there is a distinction between real and fictitious commodities, and relates this to the role of the price system in allocating resources.

The roots of this are to be found in the socialist calculation debate in the 1920s in Vienna. On one side, there was a group of socialist thinkers who thought it was possible to calculate future needs and demands without the duplication of unnecessary competition and waste. The idea was that you could build a big enough computer, input all the relevant data and plan rationally for future needs and wants. This was the basis of a planned socialist economic system. On the other side was a group of economists around Ludwig von Mises, including Friedrich Hayek, who argued such a thing was impossible. This was because the decentralized process of the price system relied on a huge amount of information that was not calculable. Price setting was a subjective process that gave a signal about what people wanted and this was essentially unpredictable and unknowable, except insofar as it revealed itself through the fluctuations of the price system. This critique of state planning, of socialist calculation, set the terms of debate for the next 100 years.

It is important to grasp the ways in which Hayek was right to appreciate the extent to which he was wrong. What is at stake is best understood through an analysis of the difference between his economic and social theory. In his social theory, he proposes three concepts that characterize the emergence of the open society, or what he calls a catalaxy. These are reason, instinct and tradition. A catalaxy, or extended economic system, is grounded in certain traditions that preserve ethics, honesty, law-abidingness, trust, skill and honesty and are irreducible to either instinct or reason. Hayek considers instinct alone a terrible threat as it is essentially communitarian and atavistic. He considers rationality alone equally threatening as it is instrumentalizing and self-defeating. Tradition is the idea he develops to mediate between and temper these two extremes of a self-defeating rationality that would lead to the 'war of all against all' and an instinct that generates a closed community.

In Hayek's economic theory, however, there is no mediating principle between the state and the market and there is no account of the institutions that uphold traditions of virtue and of trust and sustain a sense of mutual obligation. There is, therefore, no attention paid to the role they play in shaping and forming the factor market of labour and those decentralized intermediate institutions that uphold skills and translate information into knowledge. These enable people to understand and adapt to change not exclusively as an external force but also as something they can understand and shape. The body politic thus plays a vital role in organizing the economy.

This is the importance of Polanyi, who rejected both statist and market orders and tried to conceptualize the decentralized institutions that could resist commodification while preserving a price system in real commodities. His argument was that the economy requires social institutions that disseminate skills, distribute knowledge and preserve the status of the person as something other than a commodity. Societal institutions, of a non-pecuniary form, renew the cultural resources, or constituents, of society, saving them from depletion and exhaustion by defying the logic of commodification and sustain the institutions which educate the person towards a notion of *internal goods* as well as external value. Internal goods are the skills necessary for the fulfilment of a specific task; external goods are the money and recognition you receive for them. Specific skills are not fungible or transferrable, but require apprenticeship and time, education and practice. There is a connection between the ethical character of the person and the incentive structures within which they work. Virtue is vital for a functioning economy. Under the rule of the state or the market, the only relevant goods are money and power and the internal goods, or virtues, are undermined and neglected.

The fatal dualism of the individual and the collective neglects that reciprocity is self-interest, broadly conceived, and the organizing principle of society. We have a mutual interest in each of us doing our work honestly, which is a matter of reciprocity and not exclusively the result of individual incentives or collective coercion.

The subordination of reciprocity, give and take, contribution and reward, to contract and redistribution, market and state, has attenuated the system of reciprocity, co-ordination and co-operation that operates through decentralized institutions that uphold a good.

Such a system preserves and applies inherited knowledge and provides beneficial constraints on exclusively self-regarding behaviour through institutional enforcement rather than market self-regulation, through internal negotiation and accountability rather than external oversight.

The economy is here understood in terms of three forms of activity: (a) contract, which involves an immediate exchange of equivalents; (b) redistribution, which requires a central state and the movement of things to the centre and then out again; and (c) reciprocity. Redistribution and contract (state and market) form a necessary part of any society, but what is required is the ability to conceive how the state and market mesh with the rebuilding of reciprocity. A common good, or covenantal economy, is concerned with a more reciprocal and equal relationship between state, market and society – a balance of power. Society is threatened as much by an over-mighty market as it is by a domineering state.

Polanyi's thesis is that in a market storm, society will resist commodification, but due to its disintegration, that takes the form of a statist nationalism. A central part of our politics is how to avoid that outcome through the building of those intermediate institutions that preserve a human status for labour, a partnership with nature and which generate belonging and contribution. The difference from an exclusively human capital approach is that these institutions are conceptualized as an inheritance, and as a public good. Rebuilding reciprocity is necessary in order to preserve trust and the sacrifice required for complex and extended forms of co-operation within a democratic polity.

From Contract to Covenant

It is better to reconceptualize human capital as 'labour', environmental capital as 'nature' and intellectual capital as 'knowledge' and as different forms of an inheritance. In other words, when thinking of productivity and human capital, we need more attention to be placed on the institutions and not exclusively on the individual.

In economic terms, we need to look at why Germany exports twice as much to Britain as it imports. One might say that the tragedy of contemporary European politics is that Germany remains misunderstood as exclusively fiscally conservative when this is only one aspect of its economic system. It is also characterized by a vocational economy in which self-organized institutions preserve and renew the traditions of a particular craft and regulate labour market entry; by regional banks that are constrained to lend within their region; by the significant representation of the workforce in the corporate governance of firms; and by the co-determination of pensions by capital and labour. In other words, it's an economy that is characterized by the plural governance of non-pecuniary institutions that uphold and embody a virtue that is irreducible to state or market definitions alone.

The paradox of contemporary European politics is that the country with the greatest degree of labour representation in its corporate structure, the most intense system of vocational interference in labour market participation, the greatest degree of constraint on finance capital in its banking system, generates the greatest value and is the most competitive within the international economy. In other words, it is the country with the least commodified markets in labour and money.

Ernest Bevin, as Foreign Minister in the post-war Labour government, facilitated a path for Germany in 1945 based upon decentralized democracy, organized labour and the balance of power within the firm while this was defeated domestically by a Fabian vision of a scientific, centrally administered system. It is of crucial importance in understanding Blue Labour that we claim the post-war West German economic system as part of our inheritance, a path untaken, a glimpse of what could have been in Britain if we had not learnt the wrong lessons from our victory, which was based upon a war economy, planning and centralization.

Labour adopted nationalization and not co-determination, centralization and not federalism, collectivism and not solidarity, but the work done within the British-occupied zone of North Rhine-Westphalia is the greatest example of Labour statecraft in action, renewing and democratizing ancient institutions, reconciling estranged interests, nurturing labour power and its representation in the governance of industry, upholding liberty at the level of the state and democracy within the economy.[3] It was a system that constrained the commodifying power of capital and the domination of the administrative state. It was that system, moulded out of the dilapidated remnants of derelict institutions and half-remembered traditions, that gave West Germany an ethical identity, prosperity and civic peace after Nazi rule.

The social market economy has been robust enough to sustain its institutional form under conditions of globalization and its practices were brokered and pioneered within the British zone. It is one of the great tragedies of European history that it did not become the basis of the political economy of the European Union, which chose globalization rather than the internationalism that inspired it. Instead, Germany's model has been weakened and is at odds with the prevailing model of the EU.

The problem we need to overcome is that economic liberalism and Keynesianism can only conceptualize the state or the market, and all forms of particular association, as at best 'cultural' or at worst 'obstructive'. That was the limit of the Third Way, which we are trying to supplant. It had no conception of the social or of democracy. It could give no conceptual status to the specificity of place and the necessity of institutions in generating virtue and value within it.

By restoring human beings, character and institutional ethos to the analysis we can conceptualize how important autonomous institutions such as universities, professional associations, vocational colleges, unions and other aspects of the body politic are in disrupting the joint sovereignty of exchange and redistribution. Redistribution alone, as a form of centralized state administration, denies the reciprocal dependencies and decentralized diversity that characterize complex systems of economic co-operation. Market exchange, in its turn, necessarily ignores the role of supply-side institutions that regulate the valorized supply of skilled persons required for productive labour. The common good requires both constraints on individual interest maximization and the avoidance of state direction. In that sense, it is a form of socialism.

The Meaning of Vocation

Of fundamental importance in changing the economic system is a re-evaluation of vocation and the institutions required to reproduce skills and the power to adapt to changes in knowledge and in markets. A body politic made up of distinct institutions which embody a good is required to uphold incentives to virtue and the reproduction of value. The role of civic institutions and ethos in the valorization of labour value, particularly vocational institutions that place a stress on the internal as well as the external rewards of work, is part of this. The concept of 'human capital' cannot quite capture what is required for transforming our 'low-wage, low-productivity equilibrium' into something better.

There has been a sharp polarization within the labour market characterized by increasing debt and stagnant wages at the lower end. Those dependent on a modest income, without inherited assets to ease their way, have found themselves as the biggest losers of the long cycle, beginning in the 1970s, of, first, inflation, then the accumulation of public debt and finally the explosion of household debt that culminated in 2008 and the subsequent growth of payday lending.[4] The degradation of work and the places where people live has been sustained for half a century in what were once the Labour heartlands.

In terms of state economic strategy, it was assumed that there would be a decline in manual jobs and an increase in transferrable skills. As Chancellor of the Exchequer, Gordon Brown, for example, predicted in a 2006 speech that there would only be 600,000 low-skilled jobs by 2020. In fact, the number of cleaners, cooks, security guards and builders has grown since that time.[5] A consensus developed that what was emerging was a 'knowledge economy', where the knowledge in question was general, abstract and transferrable. This then grew into the idea of the 'creative economy', in which the mobile, the literate and the 'creative' were the basis of productivity growth and prosperity and state policy were based on increasing their number.

The channelling of national resources into higher education was paralleled by the collapse of the apprenticeship system, which fell from 250,000 apprentices in 1973 to 50,000 in 2016. There are, in contrast, 2.54 million undergraduates. The key moment in the humiliation of vocation as an educational practice was the transformation of the polytechnics into universities in 1992. In the meantime, despite increases in funding and multiple reforms, there has been little improvement in the educational attainment of the bottom quarter of school students. Among this population, 18% leave school without the most basic qualifications, many illiterate and innumerate. Cognitive ability overshadowed character, practical competence or experience as a criterion for success. State policy in regard to mediating globalization through a national system was based not on the reproduction of skills but on the generalization of knowledge.

One might say that the human desire to earn and to belong has not been a part of the approach and the result is that a polarized labour market has been paralleled by a volatile politics that has led to a mass defection of working-class people from Labour.

The meaning of vocation is itself a challenge to the assumptions underpinning globalization. First, it assumes a tradition of practice inherited from the past and transformed in each generation by changes in knowledge, technology and practice. In that sense, it is not entirely owned by the individual in the form of a career, but is joined by means of an apprenticeship. The distinction made in the 1830s between a profession and a vocation was decisive in the degradation of vocation as a practice. Professions required an extensive apprenticeship, induction and acculturation combined with control over labour market entry. In the process of instituting this system, certain vocations, such as medicine, law, dentistry and accountancy, were elevated in their status through legal recognition of the practices validated by the partnership between universities and professional associations and recognized by the state. This was not the fate of skilled manual labour, whose status was abolished and whose conditions were deregulated.

The professions renew their knowledge and innovate by assimilating change into an existing practice and body of knowledge. The degree of expertise and specialism is incapable of being grasped by a centralized state. Change is based on internal rather than external judgement, but it is also incapable of being sustained by a contractual economy alone. It requires institutions, such as vocational colleges, which preserve and renew the inheritance embodied in them. These resist the commodification of the practice and the person and embody the principle of reciprocity through which benefit is practised over time by mutual contribution to a common institution that sustains knowledge and status. Vocational institutions preserve bodies of knowledge and patterns of structured co-operation by adapting to the demands of external change in terms of technology, administrative rules and knowledge by translating those external dangers and possibilities into a communicable language of skills and practices. They facilitate a comprehensible adaptation to a changed environment. Vocational institutions, characterized in this way, are embodiments of human meaning and purpose, an active means of integrating new knowledge with existing practice, translating information into knowledge of a specific practical kind.

As well as its institutional inherited form, there are three other aspects of vocation worthy of mentioning. The first is that of a calling, a person finding their fulfilment and meaning in their labour, which is specific to them and not transferrable. It is not fungible. The second is the role that vocation plays in modernization. We work with a notion of modernization that denies tradition, historical inheritance and local practice in the name of a disembedded rationalism. The third is the relationship of vocation to virtue, defined by Alasdair MacIntyre as 'an acquired human quality the possession and exercise of which tends to enable us to achieve those goods which are internal to practices and the lack of which effectively prevents us from achieving any such goods'.[6]

This draws attention to the two definitions of economy, the formal one of the rational application of the minimum effort for the maximum gain – economizing – and the other substantive definition being the satisfaction of needs through combined effort. Davide Arcidiancono et al. have developed this very well through the idea of the foundational economy, which has also been called the everyday economy.[7]

The argument presented here is that through the public recognition of vocational institutions which preserve and teach the practices of specialized disciplines, defined by their own internal goods of quality and expertise, the capacity of the economy to innovate and adapt to changes in its environment is enhanced. They serve as a source of ethical regulation and expertise within the economy, and thus serve as an alternative to an exclusive reliance on external regulation. The paradox is that labour market flexibility is a cause of uncompetitive production. Or productivity is low because the status of labour is weak.

This is because productive and resilient economic activity requires a society characterized by robust non-market institutions entangled within the economy that are best described as vocational. These are based on the preservation of practices and skills through the upholding of institutional authority within the economy. This is done through the granting of work licences which permit the practice of a trade or profession through the fulfilment of an apprenticeship. This insight is most relevant for the demoralized lower end of the economy, where the degradation of work is most acute. Some notion of tradition and inherited knowledge mitigates against a revolutionary conception of change, in technology, management or production. It is on the basis of existing knowledge that the changes resulting from innovation can be assimilated. Innovation, in this sense, is the capacity to reorder and connect received ideas in different combinations rather than an exercise in making something out of nothing.[8] Amidst all the discussion of robots and technology, they can only function if there is enough expertise existing within a firm to repair, retool, redesign, reset and maintain them.[9]

It is at the point of production or delivery that quality is built into the product. Mark Elam puts this well: 'All the information inscribed in textbooks, journals, reports, data bases, patents, blueprints, standards, instruction manuals and so on, is just so much "empty talk" unless it is brought to life and lived in and out by skilled individuals.'[10] A good society, defined here as a society capable of producing goods, requires institutions within the economy that preserve the skills and practices required for concerted responses to innovation and uncertainty.[11] Vocational institutions preserve good practice, or virtue, within the culture of production by upholding the authority of civic institutions and resisting the commodification of the person and of knowledge.[12] The German economy, for example, benefits from a strong artisan sector in which vocational institutions enforce their qualifications and forbid industrial firms entering the artisanal domain. Cities and municipalities actively support, through funding and endowment, the preservation of the colleges and artisan guilds. Through the preservation of non-contractual organizations that uphold values other than the maximization of economic advantage, an ethos of production has been preserved which bestows a considerable competitive advantage in open markets. Free trade does not require a free market in labour. Or, to use the categories developed in chapter 2, through regulating the supply side in fictitious commodities, the demand for real commodities is capable of fulfilment.

It was the lack of market penetration in the formation of labour markets that bequeathed a comparative advantage to West Germany in renewing its productive methods. This is the argument of Paul Hirst when, writing about the German car industry, he says that: 'Social continuity has provided the stability and support to absorb and promote radical change in technology and economic organization.'[13]

This notion of a vocational economy requires certain institutional and legal features. The establishment of a living wage is a necessary starting point for forbidding the public bad of poverty wages. Another feature is the status of vocation in regulating labour market entry. This, however, is forbidden in an 'open' economy as a constraint on freedom of movement. Understanding this is fundamental to the tension in our economy which could be conceived as a conflict between the forces and relations of knowledge. The forces of knowledge are defined by intellectual copyright, managerial prerogative and knowledge markets. The relations of knowledge are characterized by the pooling and sharing of knowledge within and between firms and the sharing of institutional support, the most important forms of which are vocational colleges, universities as well as open access on the internet. If an information regime is imposed that prohibits the provision of public goods and conceives of vocational practice as a constraint on trade, then the productive capacity of the economy to innovate from within is threatened. This is relevant to our economy not only in terms of the traditional vocational trades of computer technology, engineering and building, but also in the growing vocations of social care, nursing, therapy and gardening.

State direction of the economy reduces virtue through its reliance on criteria external to the practices of production and is inhospitable to the demand for decentralized adaptation generated by the volatility and unpredictability of demand and technological change. The state has a vital supply-side role in the recognition and support of institutions which promote public goods within the economy. The creation of vocational colleges, which would also regulate the practices of manual trades and the legal recognition of vocations on an equal footing with professions, follows from this.

The Banks of England

In the post-war economy, capital has centralized with the same intensity as the state and this has left regions without autonomous financial institutions.

A plausible description of the British economy is that it is Portugal in the north with Singapore in the south. In terms of the body politic, there are regions of the country that are suffering from malnutrition, if nutrition is measured in terms of the inheritance of a civic ecology of assets, capital and local institutions. There needs to be a greater availability of capital within the regions and this is best pursued through the endowment of regional banks.

The British financial services sector is made up of two distinct systems: a global system centred on the City of London which provides global financial services; and a national system providing services to domestic companies. The global entrepôt hub is the principal organizing centre for global finance; in contrast, the domestic and regional financial sector has been in decline for several decades and does a poor job of supporting households and firms.

Manufacture is far more complex and demanding than financial services. It involves the material movement of things, complex supply chains and skilled labour and is far more prone to disruption. The rates of return are lower in production than in global investment. This partly explains the extraordinary concentration of capital that was revealed in the crash of 2008.

On the surface, Britain has an extremely strong financial services sector, which contributes significantly to growth, jobs and productivity in the wider economy. On most measures of financial depth, Britain scores highly. Its banking sector assets in relation to GDP, at almost 400% in 2019, are higher than any country other than small offshore financial islands, which are often linked to the City of London. Its stock market capitalization, at around 110–20% of GDP, is among the highest in the G7, behind only the United States; and the stock of corporate bonds outstanding has grown rapidly over recent years.

The size of the British financial services sector is, at least in part, the result of comparative advantage and of a long-term historical pathway. Britain runs a large trade surplus with the rest of the world in financial services, amounting to around 3–4% of GDP, without which the current account deficit would be closer to 10% than 5%.

If we look beneath the surface of these numbers, however, a somewhat different picture of the sector emerges. This derives from the fact that, as noted, the British financial services sector, in practice, comprises two distinct systems: a global eco-system, centred on the City of London, and a local eco-system. This is not surprising. The City of London, founded by the Romans, was part of their extended maritime trade system incorporating Ostia, Piraeus and Marseilles, and was open to the sea, but they built the largest city wall in Europe to protect it from domestic pressures. From Roman times, there were two distinct economic systems: the territorial and the maritime. The domestic economy was strictly regulated; maritime trade was adventurously mercantile.

The distinction between the formal and the substantive economy or the territorial and maritime economy was a central tenet of classical statecraft. Ports were placed at a distance from cities, for the sea was a place not only of tempestuous threat and piracy but also of tremendous wealth and speculation. The returns from the domestic territorial economy were always lower than those built around long-distance voyages and insurance. The basis of the British Empire was the City of London as the hub of an oceanic maritime economy every bit as much as the Roman Empire was built around the port of Ostia and the control of the Mediterranean. The distinctiveness of maritime trade is that it was based on commodification, in which everything, from people to precious stones, had a price. In the domestic economy, neither nature nor human beings were commodities and the rates of return on investment were thus constrained. In this, the necessities of life were secured without an exclusive reliance on the price system through a range of local and national measures.[14]

The City of London Corporation is the oldest continuous civic democracy in the world. As a City from 'time immemorial', it is not subordinate to Parliament and has never been required to disclose its assets. The maritime interest was an important part of the formation of the English and then the British polity, expressed in the primary role of the Navy and the Treasury, but it was constrained by Parliament and royal prerogative as well as by common law and customary practice. It was urged to keep its attention overseas and not interfere too much in the domestic economy or its politics.

The tension could not hold and there was an explosion in the 1830s when a combination of enclosures, the abolition of apprenticeship laws and the Poor Law Reforms meant that the rules of the maritime economy were for the first time enforced on dry land in the form of a free market in people, land and food.[15] Once again, democratic politics was the means through which this was constrained and refashioned through new labour market and welfare legislation as well the enforced preservation of common lands through parks and commons. What has become known as municipal socialism was an extraordinary burst of creative energy that both preserved and created civic institutions that defended the non-commodity status of people and land.

Rates of return have always been higher in the financial rather than the productive sector, in the maritime rather than the territorial, in the global rather than the national economy. The pressures of globalization are not new. A land-based settled economy is always more sluggish, in terms of the rate of return, than the mercantile maritime one. Recent research by both CRESC and the Bank of England indicates that a 'foundational economy' made up of 85% of economic activity plods along, more or less impervious to the global demands of relentless innovation and ever higher rates of return.[16] This is constituted by health, social care, relational support, local services and companies as well as building and maintenance.

As the rewards of finance are higher than those of production, and as the process of commodification raises profits and the speed of returns on investment, it also centralizes and concentrates ownership. What is required is an institutional counter-movement to resist this centralization of ownership in the City of London and the ownership of capital by fewer people. This is the fundamental political issue, and the Labour movement, organizing across race and between regions, is the indispensable force in pursuing that.

Despite the rapid growth and large scale of banks' balance sheets, there has been no discernible improvement in the availability of financing allocated to small to medium-sized British companies compared to a generation ago. This is also unsurprising. The fraction of British banks' balance sheets devoted to financing companies has experienced a fall for many decades. Capital has centralized with the same intensity as the state and this has left regions without finance or financial institutions. The story of Northern Rock is instructive in this regard.

The Northern Counties Permanent Building Society was established in 1850 in Newcastle. It was modest in its spending and embedded in the life of the region, to the extent that during the 1984 miners' strike it suspended mortgage payments so that its members could keep their homes. It was part of the local economy and society, that most precious civic inheritance, a trusted financial institution. In 1965, it merged with another local institution, the Rock Building Society, to become Northern Rock Building Society.

It demutualized in 1997 and became simply Northern Rock, which sponsored Newcastle United Football Club and became the fifth biggest lender in the British market. A mutually owned institution which had partnered its region in good times and bad for 147 years, which had weathered four serious depressions and emerged stronger from each, could not last through New Labour's period in government. It was nationalized in 2008 and Newcastle United came to be sponsored by Wonga, a company that began its lending at 4,000% at a time when the banks were borrowing at less than 3%. The club is now sponsored by a Chinese betting company. It is understood locally as dispossession and disinheritance.

Some of this may reflect the centralization of financial decision making among most banks and, in many cases, their physical disappearance from the high street. Between 1989 and 2016, 53% of British bank branches closed. At the start of the twentieth century, there were more than 7,000 British bank branches, with the local bank manager a figure of prestige and standing in the local community. Whereas once there were small platoons of local lending officers, with institutional autonomy, local relationships and power in their locality, today decision making is often automated and usually centralized. Barclays is a case study in this.[17]

The most pressing issue for a renewed political economy is how best to reconstitute and decentralize capital in the regions that have had their assets sucked into the City of London and lost in the crash of 2008.

What is required is the endowment of regional banks, called here the Banks of England, established in each city and county of Britain, which would be constrained by charter to only invest within the area within which they are established. It would have two functions:

1 investing in regional small and medium-sized enterprises, with perhaps targeted regional sub-funds with weights inversely related to regional GDP (these would be embedded in the foundational economy and would partner in establishing city and county stock exchanges);
2 the building society or local bank function of reconstituting relational and low-cost personal loans as an alternative to payday lenders.

The use of 10% of the total cost of the bailout of 2008 would provide a substantial endowment, paid for by the banks and redistributed in the form of a shared asset to the cities and counties of the country. The cost of the bailout was £137 billion, within a guarantee of £1.2 trillion.[18] This share of £13 billion would be an adequate starting point and match the scale of the depletion of capital and generate investment in the abandoned towns and counties. It would be a British form of a sovereign wealth fund: a shared asset that underpins financial stability by guarding against excessive centralization and bringing an asset to the regions that would renew its civic corporations, engage with local circumstances and be under the control of local stakeholders rather than state direction.

The corporate governance of this institution would include the Bank of England, representing the asset, as well as core anchor institutions from the city or county such as universities and hospitals, as well as elected representatives from the workforce to provide a balance of interests, accountability and a responsiveness to local needs.

The establishment of a new civic ecology, which is not

dominated by the demands of either capital or the state, and is built around an embedded self-governing corporation with a specific purpose to fill the gaps highlighted by the 2008 crash, would be consistent with the practices and principles of the economic model developed in this chapter. These include the rediscovery of place, institutions and tradition in a renewed political economy that encourages markets in real commodities and not in the commodity fictions of labour, land and money.

Restoring the Body to the Corporation

There is a widespread recognition that the prevailing form of capitalist accumulation is degraded, in terms of reward, effect and reputation. One of the reasons for this is the unilateral nature of power within the contemporary corporation, which places a primacy on shareholder return and diminishes accountability to other aspects of the corporate body. The corporation is no longer conceived of as a self-governing institution constituted by its various mutually dependent parts as befits its status as a civic body but as a cash machine based upon profit maximization. It has contracted out its body.

The processes that work, throughout the contemporary economy, to exert pressure on the corporation to act in this way define globalization. Of importance is the centralization and concentration of capital and the pressure of financialization, the necessity of finding new markets and of profit maximization, of the nationalization of risk and the privatization of reward. This leads to the intensification of commodification, in which human beings and their natural environment are turned into factors of production in the form of labour, land, housing and food markets subject to fluctuating prices with the assumption of fungibility between the different factors.

Both banking and vocation have been analysed, and in this section the power structure of the firm, its corporate governance, will be examined and the ways in which it could be rendered more accountable, reciprocal and productive. Unilateral power has a tendency to corruption and self-reward. This is not restricted to the economy. The same is true of politics and societal institutions. Accountability to different parts of the body corporate is vital for its effective functioning.

The Green Paper on Corporate Governance Reform published in 2016 stated that 'executive pay had become increasingly disconnected from both the pay of ordinary working people and the underlying long-term performance of the company'.[19] The average pay of a CEO was £1 million in 1998 but had risen to £4.3 million in 2015, down from a peak of £4.75 million in 2011. In 1998, the FTSE CEO pay ratio in comparison to the workforce was 47:1; in 2010 it was 132:1.[20] The polarization and hollowing out of the labour market was intensified by a public policy built around the administrative state and the financial sector. This model climaxed in the financial crash of 2008.

The conception of a firm as being ultimately and exclusively a monetized entity controlled by its owners remains a fundamental assumption of economic theory and practice. The conception of an economic concern that is neither private nor public eludes our political imagination, but that is precisely what a corporation is.

It is worth briefly reviewing the history of corporate governance in Britain and how we arrived at our present impasse.

Corporate governance is the set of arrangements that determine a company's objectives and control how rights, obligations and decisions are allocated within it.[21]

Corporation means body, and the establishment of a corporation initially required a Royal Charter or Act of Parliament. As self-governing bodies governed by their members, corporations are guided in their mission by their charter and its reference to their purpose.

The decisive change, generated by a series of business failures and the subsequent destitution of directors, was the emergence of limited liability in 1855. The central dilemma emerging from this was that if managers were no longer personally liable for failure, what interest did they have in protecting investors' money?

The resolution of this principal/agent problem was that the high risk carried by shareholders gave them the strongest possible incentive to safeguard the interests of the company. Without shareholder constraint, managers would have incentives to corruption, defined as the private use of public goods, and pursue their interests at the expense of the company. The conflict was resolved by aligning shareholder and managerial incentives in that remuneration simply needed to be linked to shareholder returns.

This, however, did not resolve the tensions within the corporation. Dispersed and disorganized shareholders found it difficult to discipline management – a problem compounded by the increasingly transient nature of share ownership. While it used to be understood that dividends rose and fell, that was no longer assumed and the preservation of share value was given a higher priority than investment in either research or expansion. Financialization was more important than productivity because the time horizons of finance were shorter than those of production. The result was that the common good, defined as the mutual benefit of the various parts of the corporate body – owners, workers and creditors – was subordinated to the benefit of the shareholders and their returns were given priority. This is to set aside the risk carried by the locality and society in general by their actions. In New Labour's Corporate Governance Act of 2006, for the first time in British history, shareholder primacy was hard-wired into a company's statutory purpose. The consequence is that private companies invest substantially more than public ones as the main-tenance of share price and its definition of assets and liabilities means that research and innovation are lia-bilities and intangible, and have no value in the model. In other words, the shareholder model has constrained investment.[22]

The meaning of 'incentives to vice' can be understood through this. The present system works by judging performance via the share price of a company, but its permanent maintenance requires the generation of sig-nificant risks, such as investing in either the workforce, research or expansion in order to enhance immediate returns and boost share price. This is what Andrew Haldane calls 'super-charged risk shifting'.[23] Leverage rose with intensity in the run-up to the 2008 crash, when the quest for shareholder returns was aided and abetted by creditors who charged a low and falling rate to the banks, further fuelling incentives to ever-greater risk, which ended up as systemic recklessness. The implications of risk shifting are doubly troubling. Not only does it generate excessive risk taking and credit creation during upswings; as importantly, it also contributes to excessive caution and a credit crunch during the downswing.[24]

Restoring the Corporate Body

The financial crash was the result of a failure of many things, but one of them was corporate governance. A comparative analysis of corporate restructuring strategy in Germany and Britain tells the story clearly. The resilience of German industry was based upon two fundamental differences with Britain, both relating to corporate governance.[25] The first was that in Germany each stakeholder interest – capital, labour and management – had access to the same information about the state of the firm and the sector and could negotiate a common response.

The German High Court ruled in 1982 that co-determination took priority over the claims of shareholders as it was a matter of 'public good' and this overruled the civil law concerning the ownership of capital by joint stock companies. This would have been a plausible outcome in British law if the principal/agent problem generated by establishing limited liability had not been resolved through share price alone.

In Germany, the governance and strategy of the firm became a matter of negotiation, as the workforce and their representatives gained a knowledge of economic performance and a practical role in the management of the economy. The workforce had interests in the flourishing of the firm and an internal expertise in the work of the firm and they carried risk, in terms of losing their livelihood if the company failed.[26] The sacrifices asked of workers were balanced by their participation in the process of production as an institutional partner.

This model of corporate governance ensures that the workforce have the information and institutional power to negotiate enterprise and sectoral strategies of renewal which do not sacrifice the status of the worker.

Given the problems generated by the inadequacy of the prevailing system of corporate governance to generate productive growth, or resolve a series of tensions between shareholders, management, workforce and creditors, it is necessary to develop a constructive alternative that can correct its weaknesses while preserving its strengths.

The constituent parts of the corporate body are capital, the workforce and the management of the firm. The basis of corporate governance reform should be that a third of the seats are reserved for capital, shareholders, banks and other creditors; another third should be elected by the workforce; and the final third should be split between the management of the firm and representatives of the local community. Each of these interests has a mutual interest in the flourishing of the firm and the necessity of reaching a negotiated settlement rather than the imposition of a unilateral decision.

This common good approach recognizes that the corporation is a body constituted by complex and mutually dependent functions, and the representation of that in the corporate governance model means that a common good of the firm can be negotiated. German industry works within a legal category of the 'equalization of the burdens' in which the burdens of decisions must be balanced between owners and workers.

These three institutional changes – the establishment of vocational colleges and an apprenticeship system for labour market entry; the endowment of the Banks of England; and changes in the corporate governance so there is a balance of interests within the firm – would challenge the domination of capital while resisting state domination and control. It would be pursued through a new civic ecology that would constrain the centralization and concentration of ownership while upholding a status for labour as a human factor of production built around the renewal of place.

4

Democratic Renewal

The cumulative consequence of first the financial crash of 2008–9, then the Brexit referendum and then the coronavirus is to clarify the contours of the new era that follows liberal globalization.

The left is prone to misunderstanding 'crisis' and 'revolution'. External shocks and internal incoherence create possibilities that are incapable of being seized. The financial crash of 2008 led to the beginning of the Conservative ascendency and ten years of austerity. What could have been a reckoning with globalization, with the failure of democratic politics to resist the relentless demand of capitalism to turn human beings and our natural environment into commodities, with the institutional malnutrition that turn places into reservations, turned out to be a defence of liberal proceduralism within the EU. Labour could not assert its leadership of the nation. It could not even articulate it.

This was intensified during the Brexit interregnum, which was resolved decisively by the Conservatives. Its immediate impact has been to transform the class basis of British politics. The Labour Party, and the left more generally, has lost confidence in both the working class and democracy and retreated increasingly to a legally enforced form of globalization. In rejecting the importance of place, relationships, the common good and the leadership of the working class, Labour is now out of relationship with its own tradition and the communities who formed and nourished it. It cannot speak of covenant, the Conquest or the Kingdom. In moving towards globalization, it has lost touch with the particular, with society and with the nation. With its stress on legal concepts such as justice, fairness and human rights, Labour is no longer the political embodiment of the labour interest. It champions an outdated formless modernism that has ceased to be embedded in the affections or interests of the common people. The reckoning has been brutal.

The consequences of the coronavirus have further defined the shape of things to come, of the new era, not by transforming things utterly, but by consolidating trends that were long-standing and which have been played out over the last two decades. Each of them is consistent with the historic commitments of the Labour movement. They constitute a new reality that is far more sceptical of liberal globalization and seeks to resist the domination of capital and unaccountable power. The importance of relationships, democracy and community is far more visible in our politics.

The first concerns the nation state as the primary force within bordered polities. The immediate response to the coronavirus within the EU was the reassertion of national controls over borders and the pursuit of national strategies of containment. The stipulations of the Lisbon Treaty concerning state aid and competition law were set aside in every European state and the European Central Bank ceased imposing any constraint on state spending. The state underwrote the wages of workers, as well as securing the production of necessities and the delivery of supplies. Issues relating to national autarky concerning food, water, energy and transportation became primary issues of statecraft and will remain so. The EU's response signified the death knell of globalization through Treaty Law.

State sovereignty was once the fundamental tenet of social democracy across Europe. It was through this that Labour could create the National Health Service in 1948. A few hospitals held out against nationalization and successfully appealed to the law to defend their autonomy. Labour simply changed the law through an Act of Parliament declaring the hospitals nationalized. Compensation was negotiated after the Bill was passed. The NHS became the central instrument for strengthening our national immune system and responding to the pandemic. National sovereignty has returned to the centre of politics.

The second key consequence of the Brexit vote, and the coronavirus, is the visibility and necessity of the working class. In the era of globalization, shelf-stackers, lorry drivers, hospital cleaners and carers were contracted out and invisible, fungible factors in which the value-added stars were creative, financial and managerial. The 'left behind' and the 'losers of globalization' had been asserting themselves over the past decade but were publicly lauded for their necessity and their bravery. The dignity of labour is no longer a nostalgic and antiquated phrase.[1] The importance of the working class to our well-being and survival is now recognized as it has not been for decades. Labour value has been reasserted. The Brexit vote and then the election of the Conservative government in 2019 revealed that the working class were still a decisive force politically and were opposed to a form of liberal globalization that assumed they were replaceable and irrelevant. Class is a crucial part of our politics.

Before the virus arrived, the Conservative government had already embraced an activist state and regionally targeted Keynesianism. They had a new class coalition to forge and remain intent on doing so. The state then committed to underwriting 80% of the wages on the payroll. A substantive role for the state in the support of workers was already established by the Conservatives' election victory and the importance of work, workers and the working class will not pass with the virus but remain a central part of the new political settlement. The meaning of working class is not a code for racial exclusion. Pakistani nurses, Nigerian cleaners, Portuguese carers and Bolton lorry drivers all risk their lives to keep things going. This should be hospitable terrain for the Labour Party and intensifies the argument made in chapter 3 relating to vocation and the dignity of labour: these people engage in practices that cannot be replaced by robots because they require compassion and empathy. The current situation has clarified a key aspect of labour, which is that it requires real physical presence and cannot be done from home.

And then there is the importance of place, of neighbours, of mutual aid and community. Globalization was committed to the untrammelled movement of people through space as directed by the demands of the market.

Belonging and attachment were viewed with suspicion by economic and political liberals.

The pursuit of globalization led to the neglect of the civic immune system based on a progressive abandonment of the truth that death and tragedy are part of life. Self-government and democratic accountability need to be strengthened along with those institutions that sustain local life and the ability to fulfil the needs of others. While the central state has underwritten the cost of economic suspension, this is unsustainable and indicates the same weakness as the economic crash of 2008–9, namely that capital centralizes even more emphatically than the state. Without the constitution of a robust civic ecology, embedded in local places, there will be no durable change. For a brief moment, the response to the coronavirus brought to light what was concealed by the ideology of globalization: the dependence on others for the preservation of life. This can only be strengthened by shared institutions that uphold the good and constrain the bad. These are matters of democratic decision and the new era could be hospitable to mutuality, association and a less exploitative relationship with nature and other people.

The civic ecology is related to the environment. The benefits of reduced travel and local production have never been more obvious. The production of food to feed local people and not export, the protection of biodiversity, the building of homes that strengthen stable communities and not developers, designed by the people who live in them and built by local people, using local materials and consistent with their ideas of beauty, are possible through community land trusts and land reform. Belonging, attachment and affection for place are aspects of the good, and conservation is not in itself reactionary. The previous era of globalization was based on the joint dominion of capital, a liberal state and the unfettered movement of people, money, goods and services. The new era will place democratic constraints on that.

'Take back control' resonated with the reality that politics had lost its power to act and that democratic decision making was increasingly irrelevant under conditions of procedural liberalism. By turning against democracy, Labour has cut the fraying ties that bound it to the labour interest. It has lost its identity as a paradoxical party that could combine liberty and democracy, conservatism and liberalism through its distinctive form of socialism, forged in working-class communities and congregations. Labour is no longer of the people, by the people and for the people. Labour has become increasingly like the Whigs, or what became the Liberal Party: moralistic, universal and abstract. It is no longer embedded in the country and embodied in its political representatives. In that sense, Labour has been liquidated.

A revival of the labour interest has to be built on the understanding that humans are meaning-seeking beings with a tendency to attachment, relationships and mutual concern. We are social beings who through our use of language and memory can negotiate a common life with others on the basis of democracy and shared liberties. Democracy is the practice through which those without money resist the domination of those who have it, and through voting make the claim that the world they live in is not wholly owned by the rich. Rights and democracy go together. Rights are a means of resisting democratic domination, but that doesn't mean that losing doesn't matter. Democracy is the way that rulers are held to account and the democratic verdict has consequences for the distribution of power and wealth within society.

For the Labour tradition, democratic politics is the principal means through which people resist the drive to the commodification of human beings, their institutions and countryside. Labour chose democracy and not revolution as a way of pursuing this and its politics was based on a coalition of human beings to preserve their humanity and inheritance from dispossession and disintegration. Democratic accountability should be the prevailing practice in all important public institutions that have power over people's lives and it is the best way of holding all elites to account. It was the power of democracy to make a decisive political decision that was at stake during the Brexit interregnum. It was about the sovereignty of law or the sovereignty of Parliament to make that law. The interregnum was resolved in favour of democratic sovereignty.

The Meaning of Democracy

In *The Prince* (1532), Machiavelli describes good political leadership as a virtuoso performance, improvised, daring and surprising, something unscripted and unpredictable in a world that is always capricious. Politics happens in real time in an environment that is beyond your control. The coronavirus is a classic example of that. A distant cloud became a storm that denuded previous plans. Machiavelli says that while half of politics is virtue, which he defines as skilful action, the other half is blind luck. This he calls *fortuna*. There are no 'cast-iron guarantees' in politics, as any political action generates unpredictable consequences and reactions. For Machiavelli, virtuous, skilful and timely action is the way you turn your fate into destiny. The action is in the reaction, and politics, he argues, is the art of acting in time. And Labour is out of time. The interregnum was a moment of reckoning which demanded bold action to resolve the intractable impasse. Labour was incapable of doing that. The financial crisis created the conditions and Brexit the opportunity but Labour could not act. It had lost faith in the power of democracy and in its voters. It lost its moment.

The uncharted waters of political change mean that improvisation is required, virtuosity even, and this is only possible within a tradition, in this case the Labour tradition as it emerged from within our national politics. This was based on the primacy of association and building institutions that were based on self-interest broadly conceived, things of mutual benefit. These were the burial and building societies, the assembly halls and night schools. They were also the unions and associations that secured a recognition of labour as human and ultimately the Labour Party itself as the representative of the labour interest in the city, district and county councils where it initially won power and then in Parliament.

It was a relational politics whose form was mutual and whose practice was democratic. It was of the people, by the people and for the people. It was also a class politics as poor people gained some respite from the free market and the Poor Law state through their combined effort. Capitalism was the revolutionary force that threatened the human form of labour, of the person and the meaning of their lives. It is for that reason that democratic politics is always partly a conservative force in that it wishes to protect society from the onslaught. The issue is not about change – that always happens – but how society handles the change, which is the task of politics, and which requires leadership, which involves coalition building, direction and action. It requires an appreciation of conservation as well as change, of modernization from within a tradition.

The previous chapter outlined the institutions required to deconcentrate capital and extend democracy within the economy. Decentralized institutions, in the form of self-governing corporations such as regional banks and vocational colleges, domesticate capital at source and worker representation on boards embeds firms in their locality. That is to be complemented by a deepening of democracy in the body politic and the accountability of elites within it. Democracy needs to be strengthened as a practice that characterizes the economy and society as well as politics.

The Meaning of Brexit

Brexit was an important historical episode because it offered two contrasting visions of the future. One was rights-based and transnational and the other placed a far greater emphasis on democracy and the nation state. One mediated globalization through an exclusive reliance on Treaty Law, the other through a politics of democratic accountability. The interregnum was broken by the Conservatives, who grasped the shape of the future and championed the priority of democracy within the nation state. They understood that the old was dead and they were the midwives of the new. By asserting democratic sovereignty, they have created the conditions that make Labour politics possible once more and open the possibility of a transformative economic and political programme. The Conservatives have played to the interests of the working class, but while Brexit proved fatal to the present ideological form of the Labour Party and its class base, it is also a necessary condition for the renewal of Labour and for a socialist economic policy that would give greater advantage and power to working people. It also opens up the possibility of democratic and civic reforms. A reimagining of the body politic is required if Labour is to lead the country once more. This would redistribute power and assets to the neglected areas of our country from which capital has fled along with its institutions. In order to do this, Labour must recognize that the era of liberal globalization is over and its assumptions are outdated.

The features of the new era are a more important role for the nation state, democracy, the working class and conservatism, understood as an affection for neighbours and an attachment to a place that is considered home. It was assumed, for more than forty years, that global markets, technological change and international treaties all demanded the frictionless movement of people, money, goods and services. There was no such thing as place, no time for tradition and democracy. The nation state was merely the regional administrator of a global system bound by rules that would secure capitalism and liberalism forever. Social mobility was measured by the distance you moved away from your Mum.

The crash, Brexit and the coronavirus pandemic have dispelled the vision of the future which defined the previous consensus. They have returned attention to the importance of place, and the role of the democratic institutions that can build a purposeful sense of local community.

Leaving the EU allows Labour to implement a radical economic programme outside of the constraints of the single market and the stringent conditions of the Lisbon Treaty concerning state aid and competition law. Labour could have won the war of position in the Brexit interregnum by leading the movement to leave and articulating the possibilities for national renewal that it opened up. It could have drawn on the position held by Attlee, Bevin, Castle, Foot, Shaw, Healey and Corbyn in their analysis of the EU as anti-democratic and pro-capitalist. Instead it became the defender of the old order and of globalization. The Labour leadership under Corbyn could not act and could not lead because it could not develop a coalition between the hubs and the heartlands. The Conservatives won more votes across all social classes in the 2019 election, but their lead was particularly pronounced among skilled and unskilled workers. The working class were alienated from Labour, they felt oppressed by that which they had created but which had become alien to them. It was not capital but Labour that the proletariat rebelled against. In order to restore its covenant with those who created it, Labour needs to rediscover its own tradition, which is a class politics based on the common good.

The Politics of the Common Good

The politics that is emerging could be summarized as that of the common good. With its stress on participation, the negotiation of conflicting interests, the primacy of pluralism and the goal of mutual interests, it addresses the weaknesses of the procedural managerialism of what preceded it with the Third Way.

The common good is based on a recognition that there are differences in our society and these are intensifying: differences of interests and beliefs; between capital and labour, religious and secular, immigrant and local, men and women. It is a pluralist politics. There are inequalities of power and wealth between groups as well as individuals and the danger is that those with an inheritance and assets will dominate those without. Capitalism has a tremendous creative as well as destructive power and it is necessary to recognize both. The idea of abolishing capital is fantastical and wrong. The fundamental role of Labour politics is to resist the imperative of capital to dominate society and constrain the possibilities of democracy. The politics of the common good, articulated by Labour from its inception, was to make the ruling class recognize labour's power through democracy, to negotiate a settlement that recognized the power of labour as well as capital. Within itself, the Labour movement was the common institution shared by Catholic and Protestant workers in deeply divided cities. It was the natural party of affection for immigrants throughout the last century who could build relationships with those already here. It brokered the common good within itself, between north and south, immigrant and local, Catholic and

Protestant, religious and secular. The Co-op buried them all.

It is by recognizing that politics is the way we create practices and institutions that enable people to live with each other under active conditions of civic peace that the virtues of the Labour tradition become apparent. It allows a civic inheritance to be passed on, but in order to do that, there must be an awareness of it. Dispossession was experienced not only by the English peasantry during the enclosures, who then had to piece together a meaningful life under conditions of extreme exploitation and exclusion, but by people from all over the world who have come to live here. Capitalism is a universal that works through commodification. Politics is a particular practice based upon the traditions and institutions that characterize cultures and places.

Blue Labour politics is based on an analysis of capitalism as an extractive system founded upon class exploitation through the process of commodification. In domestic application, it was an attempt to dehumanize and dispossess the peasantry. In imperial application, it was based upon the imposition of property rights that used racial and ethnic categories that combined oppression with exploitation. The rejection of racial segregation, and the active building of a multi-racial coalition built around class and place, is a vital part of our politics.

This is expressed domestically and internationally through the politics of non-domination and reciprocity. It allows for political decisions to be made that benefit the poor and the excluded but on the basis that they organize their politics and represent themselves. That is Labour politics. The contemporary Labour Party has increasingly seen its mission as giving a voice to the voiceless and has forgotten that they can speak for themselves.

Community Organizing

The practices of community organizing are of vital importance in the rediscovery of that politics. It is founded upon the traditions developed within Labour and trade union organizing based upon building relationships between divided communities so they could act on matters of common concern; developing leaders from within the working class and engaging in action agreed from within a common organization. Underpinning this is the idea that there are three kinds of power: state power, money power and relational power.

State power refers to the coercive apparatus of the collective state; money power to the resources that ownership of capital confers to buy people and influence. Against this the only power working people have is relational power: the power to associate and work together in building organizations that can represent their interests on matters of mutual concern. This is what organized labour used to do in the period of its growth. This is related to the co-operative tradition, which is based upon building institutions of mutual aid, such as burial and building societies. Community organizing is a politics of democratic accountability, in which the state and market are held accountable to the people they serve. It is also a politics in which interests, power and leadership play a central role.

Mutual interests are discovered through building relationships between estranged communities who live in close proximity in urban conurbations. For more than ten years, I was involved with the Living Wage campaign led by the East London Communities Organization, known as TELCO, which then became London Citizens and which is now Citizens UK. In this, contracted-out cooks, security guards and cleaners, the ones who were no longer invited to the Christmas party and belonged to no union, and who were overwhelmingly from immigrant communities, played a leading role.

The immigrant workers had far greater trust in their faith institutions than in the political and civic institutions that were the main carriers of politics, such as the political parties or the trade unions. Based on the political method of organizing developed by Saul Alinsky in Chicago in the 1940s, organizers built relationships, mainly but not exclusively between faith communities, and developed leaders within them. They did this through a combination of extensive one-to-one conversations and leadership training which taught the importance of relational power as a means through which poor workers could negotiate a better life and resist the domination of money and the state.

The Living Wage campaign itself emerged out of conversations between different faith congregations: Catholic, Muslim and a variety of Protestant denominations. The dignity of labour, the obligations of love and the need for rest were tenets held by each of the faith traditions and they found common cause on an issue that directly affected their lives, namely the compulsion of finance capital to turn what was not produced for sale on the market, human beings, into a commodity, a factor of production, to be exploited and discarded due to the imperative of maximizing returns on investment at the highest rate and the greatest speed. This went under the name of 'contracting out'. The conversation between the faiths had led to a radical political economy based upon quite conservative social assumptions: the importance of family, work and the preservation of a human status for workers.

What was held sacred between the communities was the dignity of work, which was being degraded, and a desire for a recognition of contribution by those who had been excluded from permanent employment and from any permanent status by their employer. The different faiths gave an ethical form to a demoralized life based on short-term contracts with no negotiating power. The battle between isolated people and concentrated capital should have been hopelessly one-sided, but as the different congregations began to organize together, they built their relationships and increased their power by acting in the world to change things. In doing so, they succeeded in asserting the importance of place under conditions of globalization. A classical conception of citizenship shared between many different secular political traditions was renewed through an affirmation of common citizenship by people of faith and this took the form of the London Living Wage. At no point was there any imposition of religion through politics, any discussion of abortion or sharia law; instead there was the building of a common politics that could hold market and state power to account.

In the Living Wage campaign, secular and faith traditions provided a shared resource to resist the domination of capital and it took the form of a secular political economy and not a desire to impose religious laws. It was pluralist and any attempt to impose a particular religious view was resisted from within.

By basing its practice on citizen participation, the Living Wage campaign generated relationships and a shared commitment to a common good between estranged communities who were otherwise competing for scarce resources in poor areas, and it developed leaders from within those communities who had a following and whose lives were transformed by the experience. The campaign almost invariably led to the end of contracting out and the restoration of the corporate body within institutions so that cooks, cleaners and security guards could expect some kind of meaningful pathway within the firm or institution. It restored some sense of a body to a corporation, and some kind of balance between its component parts. It was a common good politics in which secular and religious, Christian and Muslim, and within that Catholic and Protestant, Sunni and Shia, universities and schools, working- and middle-class people could work together on a shared conception of citizenship that was led by those who were previously powerless and who now, through building relationships, could hold accountable those with power over them. It was also a common good politics because it combined immigrants and locals and brought perspectives and traditions relating to justice and democracy from all over the world.

Place-based community organizing begins with establishing relationships, not bringing people into an already agreed agenda, and, through negotiation, allows for the development of a politics that is owned by local people. It is a form of social democracy in that it rebuilds society.

Statecraft, the Nation State and Parliament

The main national forum for hammering out the common good, in a way that was championed at a local level by the East London Communities Organization, is Parliament, but Parliament needs reform. The paradox of the House of Lords is that as an unelected chamber it does not challenge the primacy of the House of Commons and underwrites the primacy of democratic sovereignty. While there is experience and expertise in the Lords, it remains a vestige of cronyism and patronage in our polity. The remedy lies not in abolition but in its transformation from within the framework of the Ancient Constitution.

The Commons is a locational democracy where Members of Parliament are elected from the place in which they live. This strengthens the importance of areas that are poor in all things but the vote. It ensures that local as well as exclusively national concerns are represented. It strengthens diversity by the direct link of MPs to those who elect them. The Lords, in contrast, as a chamber which amends and advises, should represent vocational democracy, where people are elected from their working lives. There should be people elected from their sector, whether that be electrical or academic, medical or administrative. Doctors should elect a peer, as should nurses and cleaners. It would give an incentive to the organization of carers, builders and cleaners, who would elect a representative from within their vocation.

Central to the Ancient Constitution is the idea of the balance of interests rather than the separation of the powers. The judges should be returned to the chamber as law lords so that it is the final court of appeal, thus restoring the balance of power in Parliament as the protectors of the common law. The vocational chamber would revise and amend legislation as it does now on the basis of the judgement of people who actually know what they are talking about and who are recognized as experts in their field by their peers through democratic election.

The move towards becoming a self-governing democracy demands that we recognize the weaknesses of the prevailing system and take steps to remedy them. The representation of the working life of society, in its myriad of vocational forms, would bring experience and knowledge where currently it is lacking. The role of the Lords is to advise, amend and suggest, so that would not interfere with the primacy of the Commons but complement it.

It would be a form of constitutional and institutional renewal that serves modern demands within the constraints of the Ancient Constitution and offers an alternative to the status quo that would be consistent with its historical form. Such an arrangement would ensure that the working life of the country is represented in Parliament, and that would be a complement to Labour as the representative of the labour interest in the Commons.

In order to redeem itself, Labour will have to draw upon submerged and neglected traditions that offer an alternative perspective to those which dominate now. It also needs to rehabilitate ancient political concepts that have fallen into misuse. One of these is the common good. Another is community organizing. A third is the commonwealth tradition, in which the polity is viewed as a common inheritance, and the political institutions that make up the body politic are an essential part of self-government and the expression of sovereignty. In this, cities, counties and civic institutions have a constitutive role to play in the democratic self-government of the country. The role of statecraft could be defined as facilitating and co-ordinating the growth of the democratic decentralized institutions required for a social democracy.

Renewing the Body Politic: the Tribunes, the County and the Parish

The Tribunes

There is a recognition that parliamentary and local elections are insufficient to secure the good governance of powerful institutions in-between elections. There is interest in citizens' assemblies as an alternative forum of debate, but it is unclear what power they would have beyond recommendations and whose interests they would serve. Of greater relevance would be forums for accountability in which democratic decisions on public appointments, and on malfeasance, are decided in local assemblies or, as they were called in Ancient Rome, tribunes.[2] Non-citizens, or the 'plebs', were allowed to call assemblies where they thought that corruption had occurred. They had the right of veto in public appointment, to remove from office, and, if proven in proper trial, to jail those who abused their power. That should be the role they play today. As Machiavelli points out in *The Prince*, the tribunes had 'teeth as well as tongue', and provided a check on a Roman elite that wished to ignore the plebs by giving them bite as well as voice. The introduction of tribunes into our politics for the public appointment of head teachers and directors of hospitals, as well as directors of businesses and banks, would bring a genuine accountability to our civic life which is absent, and a real power to those who are affected by decisions. It would function alongside Parliament without challenging its political authority. It would be a guard against corruption but also make civic and public institutions accountable to those they serve and correct them when they fail.

Machiavelli pointed out that while our rulers are motivated by a desire to dominate, the 'common people' just don't want to be oppressed. The tribunes would provide a civic forum through which they could debate and discuss appointments that concern them directly and give a genuine accountability which could judge in cases of corruption. The story of Stoke Mandeville Hospital is a classic example of a lack of local accountability.[3] The establishment of tribunes would provide a vital institutional link between the rulers and the ruled. Holding the leaders of our public institutions to account engages fundamental interests for those who go to hospital and whose children go to school and are affected fundamentally by their leadership. If there are serious problems, an assembly could be called if 1,000 people were to sign up for it. This is the sphere in which community organizing could play a vital role in embedding public institutions in the life of the localities they serve.

The County and the Parish

Only those institutions that enjoy affection excite the political imagination. It is an extraordinary fact that more people describe the place where they live in terms of the 1536 parish map than they do the administrative map of 2022. Medway, Humberside or the West Midlands are the objects of no affection. The restoration of the ceremonial county as a unit of self-government would work within the affections of people. It would have responsibility for the rivers, the roads and the track that runs through it with powers to pursue distinctive policies on the environment and housing. The county hundred was the old system of government and was based on property ownership and status. The modern county hundred should be elected by the people of the county as a council and they would elect their sheriff.

There should also be a redistribution of power to the smallest unit of self-government. The parish is an elemental aspect of our polity, ecclesiastical and temporal. The parish, the county, the town and the city remain the fundamental units of affection, attachment and affiliation. The parish remains consistent with where people think they live. It is small enough to be a community of people who recognize each other in the street without knowing who they are. The logic of globalization is to disrupt and erase a sense of belonging, to displace space. It is predicated on universal procedures that require unmediated movement and are hostile to the constraints of institutions with tongue and teeth.

The parish commune, as a site of secular power, should be based on the participation of all people within the parish in the form of a local assembly. Such a council system has been developed in north-eastern Syria, or Rojava, under the leadership of the Kurdish YPG and provided a politics of the common good between communities that was central to the defeat of ISIS. The parish commune is consistent with the necessity of restoring a sense of place, of a home in the world where people can participate in their own democratic self-government. If it decided matters of housing, land reform, education and policing, there would be real power at play.

The menace and the promise of democracy would be part of people's lives. Relationships can be established and leaders developed within local communities. The origin of the hustings lies in the parish and it has endured as a locational focus of identification even when it has had no political relevance. The revival of the parish would also give church buildings a continued importance that would be consistent with their historic role. Persecuted people found refuge at the church door. Democratic renewal would be deepened by the autonomy of the parish commune as the elemental unit of local self-government.

Underlying this is a sense of the *vita activa*, of active citizenship, that is a necessary part of a democratic way of life in which we actively negotiate our common existence and have the power to decide its form. The ideology of globalization is based on the centrality of the internet, of online shopping and Netflix. Unlike the parish council, which has very limited powers, the parish commune would be a direct democracy in which issues of immediate concern to residents could be addressed and voted upon. In this way, the parish becomes an elemental unit of political self-government, and through it the mutual dependence of people on a shared civility could be learnt once more. The vitality of democracy would become part of local life.

Blue Labour

The Fate of Social Democracy

These Labour traditions could renew democracy, a social democracy. The travails of the left, however, go beyond Britain. Across Europe, social democracy has no concept either of the social or of democracy. That is the cause of its continental palsy. It became increasingly reliant on the state while promoting a global regime that denied the state any effective economic agency. Its stress on the primacy of procedural justice subordinated civic institutions, the social to the state, while opening up what was left of society to transnational corporations. Democratic resistance to this was made effectively illegal across the EU.

It was the historic role of the European social democrats to resist the domination of capital by strengthening democracy and upholding liberty. That was its fundamental break with communism. Unlike communism, social democracy did give a leadership role to the working class and a primacy to their interests within the polity. The sovereignty of the nation state was fundamental to this. Social democracy has destroyed the social and subordinated democracy. It can only be renewed if it restores the primacy of both. Labour avoided – at least for a time – the fate of its European comrades, who have been moved to the margins of national politics. In the 2017 General Election, it did this by 'respecting the result of the referendum'. By 2019, it had abandoned that principle and it was rejected.

It need not be this way. The restoration of national sovereignty will reach its limit at the market, where the sovereignty of capital makes its demands, and they will increase. The Conservatives understand neither the voraciousness of capital nor the role of democracy in domesticating it. It is the role of Labour to lead the democratic resistance to that, to the clauses in trade deals that allow the commodification of human beings, nature and our public institutions, to challenge the limits of democratic sovereignty within the economy and polity. That is the point of democratic sovereignty, and that is the point of Labour. It pursues a social democracy and its orientation is internationalist.

5

Internationalism versus Globalization

A Change of Era

Pope Francis said in 2019 that we are living not in an era of change but in a change of era. The contours of the new era are characterized by an increased role for the nation state and democracy as well as a recognition of work and workers as something other than fungible and replaceable units of production. The new era has all the ingredients to be dehumanizing, disembodied and authoritarian, but it could also be more sociable, democratic and free. Whether it goes one way or the other depends on the type of politics that we pursue and the allies that we make.

The class coalitions underwriting our party politics were reconfigured around the issue of the nation state and globalization and the realignment took the form of Brexit.[1] There were those who thought that globalization could be best mediated through membership of the EU and those who thought it was through a sovereign nation state. The interregnum was resolved in favour of the latter.

The dynamics of domestic politics shape the direction of foreign policy and this should be organized around the pursuit of a democratic self-organized society based on the liberties of association, expression, conscience and religion. The primacy of capital within the constitutional framework of the EU led, in Britain, to a rejection of treaty-based globalization in favour of democratic decision. The definition of the national interest by finance, the notion that our prosperity rests on the City of London, is also being challenged. The United States is no longer the undisputed champion of globalization, or the unilateral hegemon of a global order built in its self-image. The framework of global order will be based on the balance of power within a nation state system. Drawing on the tradition of internationalism frames the argument that this should be characterized by non-domination, reciprocity and coalition building, with a primary role for the non-commodity status of labour and nature. This is consistent with the idea of self-interest, broadly conceived, developed in chapter 1.

The goal of our foreign policy is defined as the defence of our institutions of democratic self-government and liberty and the building of alliances with those with mutual concerns. The status of labour and nature as non-commodities is central to this. It requires co-operation with other people to uphold common goods. This requires a redefinition of the national interest away from an exclusive concern with trade and money, most particularly finance. The shadow of our imperial past is cast by the invisible earnings of the City of London, which remains the hub of a global financial system that has atrophied our industrial capacity at home and dominated our reputation abroad.

The structure of the modern British state was in many ways given by the domination of the financial interest within our polity. The historical primacy of the Navy within the armed forces and of the Treasury within government were driven by securing sterling as the reserve currency and the freedom of the sea within a maritime imperium. The definition of imperialism used here is the imposition of a trading and legal system on subjugated territories. In the formation of Empire and after its dismantling, the promotion of free trade within a global maritime system, with the City of London at its hub, has been the primary goal of foreign policy. This, however, does not equate with the national interest. It has certain aspects that should be strengthened – a preference for peace and the pursuit of a balance of power – but it was ultimately weighted in favour of capital, and the labour interest, as well as democracy, were subordinated to rates of return. This is the deep story of the present crisis. The penetration of the market into all aspects of society is unsustainable and undermines a stable economy and polity as well as civic associations.

The Meaning of Globalization: the Priority of Capital over Labour

At the basis of globalization was the reassertion of the rights of capital and a corresponding diminishment of those of labour. The post-war settlement, brokered by the Labour government after 1945, hindered and stymied the sovereignty of finance through all manner of controls and restrictions that meant it had to reach a settlement with a workforce that had strong institutional and political representation. This was based not only on nationalization but also on trade unions playing a significant role in the private sector. This meant that workers could negotiate pay, with guarantees of job security, pensions and benefits through organized labour and the threat of strikes. One of the foundational aspects of the New Right critique of the post-war settlement in the 1970s was that the principal cause of stagflation, the fall in profits and the 'crisis of governability' was that trade unions had crossed the line and were sabotaging both government and the economy. This is what had to be changed.[2]

The victory of Margaret Thatcher in 1979 unleashed the City of London on the world. The de-industrialization of the North and the Midlands was based upon relocating production to China, where the rate of return on investment was higher and faster because the workforce was plentiful, cheap and diligent. This was backed by the host state through sustained infrastructure projects and guarantees of continuous production.

The alternative to this is a national economy based on a decentralized system of institutional constraints. This would renew a politics of place and embed the economy and government in local systems of societal accountability.

This is complemented by internationalism, which, unlike globalization, is based not on the unimpeded movement of capital, goods, services and labour as commodities, but on a recognition of the threat to the human status of the person by capitalism and a reassertion of the social nature of human beings and the non-commodity status of nature as an inheritance and a trust. It gives a central place to both democracy and freedom of association.

As globalization fractures, it is vital to develop a form of internationalism that is based not on the mutual impoverishment of workers but on a protection and enhancement of their status. The relationship between the change in domestic consensus and the international order has not been explored adequately within Labour or within the left more generally, as under New Labour liberalism trumped socialism and globalization replaced internationalism. Over the last two decades, Labour has not given serious consideration to how to uphold the labour interest and the specific role that Britain could play in establishing a different international settlement. A space has opened up for a new internationalism that could tip the balance in favour of workers and democracy within a framework of new alliances.

The post-war order was the great achievement of Labour internationalism. The United Nations, the World Health Organization, the World Bank, the International Monetary Fund and NATO were all championed by the Labour government, with Ernest Bevin as Foreign Secretary. This was initiated with the establishment of the International Labour Organization by the League of Nations in the Treaty of Versailles in 1919, which was rolled over into the United Nations in 1948.

The establishment of the particular institutions of the West German economy, the trade union representation in corporate governance and pension funds, the vocational regulation of the labour market and the decentralized regional banking system were all established initially in the British zone of North Rhine-Westphalia before being established nationally with the constitution of the

Federal Republic. This gave labour an elemental role in the governance of the economy and deconcentrated capital. The decentralized German system has been far more effective than our centralized model and there are huge strengths in the system we championed abroad but did not adopt at home.[3] If the German model had served as a basis of the EU, it would have been an internationalist rather than a globalizing institution. As it stands, many of those German achievements were undermined by the neoliberal Hartz reforms under Gerhard Schroeder in the early 2000s, which exacerbated inequalities in the labour market, and the embrace of the EU as a Hayekian single market in which organized labour had no role. The social market economy was not articulated as a viable model for the EU. Germany remains dominant, but not hegemonic, and that is the tragedy of contemporary Europe.

The Disintegration of Globalization

The two pillars of globalization, the United States and China, are no longer aligned, and this has generated a new form of imperial rivalry within an aggressive and combustible nation state system. Iran and Pakistan have already allied with China in this new configuration.[4]

The relationship with China has emerged as the dominant conflict of the post-globalization period, intensified by the coronavirus. A variety of voices in the Conservative Party have expressed concern on issues ranging from Huawei's participation in the development of the 5G network to Chinese firms buying the British steel industry to Chinese investment and access to Hinckley Point with a strategic role in the development of our nuclear energy system.

At no stage is it mentioned that the increasing domination of China and its powerful role within the global economy has been achieved through the active partnership with western capital, which was based on political decisions taken over the last forty years to diminish the power of labour in our economy and polity. While Britain pursued the mirage of the 'knowledge economy', China maintained a strategic industrial policy with a central role for manufacturing and this is what has led to our dependence on it in chemicals, medicine, industrial parts and technology, including renewables. In both Britain and the United States, it was a class-based policy with capital pushing for the coalition with China. The CCP wanted access to technology and capital, business, cheap labour and a new market. China welcomed and absorbed the new investment with a coherent industrial policy that included central and local government grants, tax exemptions, subsidized land, cheap energy and low-interest loans from both public and private banks. And China underwrote the increasing western debt.

China is the principal threat to our democracy and liberty because of its industrial power and its ideological commitment to a form of state capitalism that has no place for either. It assigns no role to the human status of labour, and there is no possibility of such a role. It is also closely aligned with capital in the form of the society it wishes to generate: a frictionless society based on human isolation and managerial domination within the framework of Party sovereignty.

The era of globalization was premised on the domination of capital over labour and based on the partnership between the City of London and the Chinese Communist Party in order to achieve that. It was an era during which the fundamental principles of statecraft relating to the provision of necessities in times of crisis, or scepticism about an over-reliance on foreign powers, were considered archaic, populist and dangerous. There is a shared structure of thought between communism and capitalism in insulating the economy from political interference as well as a collusion of interests.

It is not just the chlorinated chickens that are coming home to roost.

The partnership with China was initially a right-wing project, from Nixon to Thatcher. It was a partnership that the New Democrats and New Labour seized upon and was elevated to a moral principle by Clinton and Blair in which millions were 'lifted out of poverty' and China was integrated as a full citizen within the 'international community'. This enshrined globalization as an inevitable *telos* and has framed policy for two decades. It was our fate and there was nothing we could do about it. China's admission to the World Trade Organization was part of this, as was the intensification of de-industrialization in Britain. This was subsequently furthered by Cameron and Osborne and their following of the 'new silk road'.

The faith in liberal globalization which characterized the New Labour years, in which free trade naturally led to democracy and liberty, was, however, revealed as a delusion. This was called 'harmonic convergence'.[5] Bill Clinton expressed the view forcefully when he argued that China's accession to the World Trade Organization would lead to 'faster and further' moves towards 'greater openness and freedom for the people of China'. The opposite is true. Not since Mao has the Party been in such a dominant position, and a policy of internal and external domination been so publicly pursued.

Globalization was built upon this alliance between western capitalism and eastern communism in order to diminish the status of western labour. The partnership between liberal economics and authoritarian one-party rule was a perfect fit. The decline in the share of GDP going to labour and the corresponding increase in the share going to capital have been constant since 1980 across all western economies and all sectors, with the exception of finance and business services.[6] The creation of global supply chains was code for the outsourcing of manufacturing jobs to the lowest-cost producer, contracting out domestic labour-intensive services and excluding unions from the private sector. The modern corporation divested itself of its body by subcontracting cleaning, security, catering and distribution through a high-churn disposable workforce. Freedom of movement was central to this. The precariat was formed and these moves were welcomed by investors. Companies that directly employed fewer people were more highly valued. The emphasis was on consumption and profit. Production, like workers, became invisible and invisible earnings became the bedrock of our economy.

The Great Transformation of the Chinese economy has been the most significant story of the era of globalization, and none of the assumptions that marked its emergence have characterized its present form. It was assumed that it would lead to a liberal democracy. The opposite has happened. Under President Xi, there has been an intensification of the surveillance state and the domination by the Party of the state apparatus. There has been a systematic subjugation of minorities, with over a million Uighur Muslims held in prison camps with enforced slave labour and the mass movement of Han Chinese into Tibet as it is turned into a macabre theme park. The freedoms of association, religion, speech and conscience are viewed as hostile to the wellbeing of the Chinese nation and belligerence towards Hong Kong and Taiwan has increased. In July 2013, a central committee document was leaked which summarizes the 'seven perils' emanating from contact with the West. These include political pluralism, civil society, freedom of the press and internet and historical research which questions the superiority of 'socialism with Chinese characteristics'. 'Xi Jinping Thought' was elevated to the level of that of Mao and Deng Xiaoping. China did not conform to progressive models of globalization. In contrast, it emerged as an alternative future in which increased prosperity, welfare and security could be pursued without either liberty or democracy.

The benefits to capital that have flowed from its exploitation of Chinese workers is necessary to bear in mind when reflecting on the role of China in the global economy. Less than 2% of the retail value of an iPhone assembled in China goes to labour while 58.5% goes to Apple as profit. Workers have twelve-hour shifts and two days off a month. Above all, they are prohibited from forming their own organizations.

China's initial role in the spread of the coronavirus was caused by the primacy of globalization in its state policy. When the coronavirus began, China banned domestic flights from Wuhan but kept international flights open. That, more than anything, turned a local plague into a global pandemic. Priority was given to the movement of people and goods rather than health considerations; membership of the World Trade Organization was prized over membership of the World Health Organization. It took the involvement of the Politburo to enforce the lockdown. Confusion of function, avoidance of blame and wishful thinking played as much of a role as systematic malice, although each were present. The form of communist government was more significant here than Chinese cultural traditions, as anyone familiar with Soviet literature on cover-ups and repression would recognize.

China was a founder member of the International Labour Organization. Central to its mandate was freedom of association and free and democratic trade unions. The People's Republic of China refused to sign the protocols relating to the freedom of association and to recognize independent trade unions in 1948 and has refused to ratify the protocols ever since. The International Labour Organization has decades of examples of intimidation, violence and threat by the Chinese authorities against those who have tried to found independent unions. The use of the Army against strikers is commonplace. This has been public knowledge for forty years. It was assumed that the benefits of the Great Transformation of the Chinese economy went to the workers, but this is not the case. Instead the workforce has been displaced, controlled, isolated and exploited, their experience shielded from international scrutiny.

The right cannot give an honest account of its complicity in the dominance of the inhumanity of the Chinese system, its return on investment is too high. The employment practices of Amazon, for example, with its surveillance of workers, ban on union organizing and preference for immigrant labour with fewer rights, is an indication that without resistance in the form of free and democratic trade unions, capitalism is an inhumane and violent system and sticks closely to the system established in China. The interests of capital have been placed above all other considerations. In the emerging era, strategic interests will require more protection, and this means that the City of London will play a lesser role in our polity. That is why both class and the common good should shape our relationship with other states.

The Wrong Side of History

In terms of internationalism, the left has been compromised in two ways. The Labour Party moved from a general suspicion of the European project in the early to mid-1970s to becoming its strongest advocate in 1997. This was caused by its abandonment of a national political economy and its embrace of globalization. There were undoubted benefits to capital and the consumer but the substantive or foundational economy was decimated. With Britain's departure from the EU, one of the chief beneficiaries of this settlement, the universities, now stands exposed to bankruptcy and compromised integrity. The domestic reckoning began with Brexit but is only now being revealed in terms of productive incapacity and exposed supply chains.

There is another tradition on the left which relishes the possibility of a Chinese future. This belongs to those who assign a central place to technology and rationality and improving the human condition within a global future in which democracy and particularity play no

131

significant role. The assumption is that the ability of a rational administration to plan for long-term growth without the selfish and short-term interests that democracy presents leads to greater public benefits. Lockdown offered a taste of such a future. It was characterized by greater use of the internet and virtual meetings, with our needs and wants supplied by Amazon and Netflix, our social life by Facebook. The displacement of place, association and politics by scientific rules and automated satisfaction. Life both abundant and bare. A frictionless society.

There are two possible futures that loom over the present crisis. One is characterized by the elimination of democratic accountability owing to both a more powerful central state and large corporations that base their legitimacy on science and rationality. They would dominate the economy and society within a global system in which the external goods of profit and market penetration subordinate the human status of labour and the integrity of the environment. The other is based far more on democracy and the defence of liberty entangled in local economies. There is an important and increasing role for the state in this, centred on the need for an industrial strategy, which has been outlined in chapter 3. There is also a need for the development of a kind of corporatism that requires the participation of capital, labour and the state. It was once known as social partnership. What is distinctive about globalization is the elimination of democracy in the representation of interests. The political decisions we make will determine which way we go. Central to this is whether we embrace globalization – with China as its chief proponent – or internationalism.

The coalition between corporate capitalism and Chinese communism is profound and will not evaporate. Both are committed to a rules-based system of trade in which democracy is subordinated to the freedom of movement of goods, services and money. Both wish to subordinate labour to capital and democracy to trading rights. Both are hostile to politics. China is now serving as a proxy for a wider system of domination by capital and the state that denies the power of association and labour as expressed through voting and free association. It is worth noting that communist rule has eviscerated the human form of labour.

Internationalism is based on the mutual interests of workers in defying their dehumanization and exploitation by capital through democratic association and politics. The fundamental means of doing this is support of free and democratic trade unions which can express the interest of labour as a human factor of production. Workers' ability to withdraw their labour enables them to negotiate with capital and force the state to defend their human status. It is also based on democracy in the polity.

The coronavirus intensified the underlying conditions that already existed. On the one hand, China had displaced Russia as the systemic alternative to the combination of liberty and democracy characteristic of the West. On the other, the nation state was returning as a more significant force, as was working-class disaffection with globalization. Common action on environmental hazards was forcing a shortening of supply chains and an engagement with the renewal of local economies. The death knell of globalization has been sounded but the new order cannot be born. We have entered an international interregnum in which there will be a fraternization of opposites and all manner of morbid symptoms will pertain.

Internationalism versus Globalization

The Labour tradition is based on internationalism rather than globalization. There are national interests relating to security, liberty, the integrity of self-government and the satisfaction of needs that are fundamental. There are mutual interests shared between nations, however, that should guide our relationships. These are fundamentally related to the balance of power, the status of labour and the environment.

The ideas of the substantive economy developed in chapter 3 are central to this.

The first step is to have a more autonomous relationship with the United States and take a lead in building a new network of alliances based on common interests. The limits of liberalism are manifest in the incoherence of the United States. This is based on its inability, as the founder of liberal globalization, to seek anything other than domination in establishing the fundamental rules of association, and to acknowledge the role of violence in its maintenance of power or the balance of interest in the maintenance of order. Above all, it is due to its inability to recognize capitalism as a violent and volatile form of economic organization.

The United States of America has been a Janus-faced country since its inception. One of its faces is that of enlightened constitutional legality, forged in 1776, moving to an ever more perfect union. In this, freedom of religion, of association, democratic federalism and individual rights play a fundamental role. It is a national republic but also a notional republic, based on the universal values of liberty and equality.

The other face is that of a specific linguistic ethnic national community who laid claim to the ownership and domination of a huge territory and the subordination of rival claims. This involved genocide, slavery, death squads, vigilantes, land seizure, depopulation and repopulation. Both faces are real and have found no means of reconciling their different conceptions of identity and power. The conception of freehold title upheld by the Constitution mean that there can be no sharing of the inheritance. The fissures of race mean that while America developed the most advanced capitalist economy, there was no corresponding national Labour Party that could resist the commodification and inequality that flowed from this. Racial, religious and regional differences undermined the several serious attempts to make class the organizing principle of a national political party. The politics of racial division stymied the emergence of a social democratic politics. The defeat of Bacon's Rebellion in 1672, in which black and white indentured labour combined to challenge the plantocracy, was decisive.[7] A racial capitalism was established that stymied the possibility of resisting the distribution of land and wealth. It was in response to the rebellion that racial laws were instituted, the first being the Virginia legal code of 1691.

The same uncomprehending bipolarity has been reproduced in the liberal order that America has led since 1945. Based on constitutional capitalism, not only did the United States ultimately join in defeating Nazism, and then the Soviet Union, it underwrote democracy in the defeated Axis countries and the establishment of international institutions of global governance. At the same time, it funded death squads and promoted coups all over Latin America, dropped four times more bombs on Vietnam that it did in the entire Second World War and was prepared to ignore Pakistani mass murder in Bangladesh in return for brokering detente with China.[8] While part of this is due to the very idea of a revolution, which severs all connection with what went before, it is also due to the incapacity of liberalism itself to understand itself as a system of violence and power, to doubt its good intentions or to understand other people and cultures who do not share its assumptions. Britain has the ability to understand tradition and history as a complex legacy and the importance of time in reconciling estranged interests. Labour has the tradition through which it can understand the violence and dispossession that capitalism involves, particularly when imposed from within an imperial structure.

After the Second World War, the United States pursued a foreign policy based on two assumptions: corporate dominance and the Cold War. Its supremacy was based upon its industrial predominance and the decimation of its rivals. It underwrote, against its inclinations, a pro-worker settlement in West Germany, but with the decline in communism, the abandonment of its industrial strength due to the partnership with China and the championing of globalization, the hollowing out of its economy and the domination of finance, the United States became hostile to labour, and organized labour in particular. Its domestic tensions are expressed through its foreign policy.[9] It has been unable to reconcile with

Russia and extricate from China, outmanoeuvred by Iran in Iraq, bound to Turkey in Syria. There is no reason to be shackled to incoherence. There are many mutual interests between Britain and the United States, but in terms of workers' ability to organize, the capacity of society to self-organize, upholding the integrity of nature and democracy, Britain can take the lead. The practice of self-government is that of internal mediation and negotiation, which requires a society that can hold both market and state to account. Corruption, violence and tyranny are permanent possibilities in politics. The only sustainable alternative is that of an organized democratic society to expose and challenge them.

The fundamental issue at stake in the conceptualization of foreign policy is to strengthen the possibility of politics, the ability to act on the basis of democratic legitimacy in a world constituted by interests. The national interest is the capacity for self-government. This confronts 'universal' interests and values which are opposed to the 'particularity' of democracy. Capitalism and market economics, it has been argued, generate greater prosperity and closer ties between people. It is, therefore, unreasonable to constrain the free movement of people, goods, services and money as it leads to immiseration and conflict. This was the fundamental argument in favour of the EU and why it is necessary to subordinate democracy to a shared framework of rights and rules that uphold individual liberty and a shared framework of production and exchange.

A similar argument is put forward in terms of environmental protection. This proposes that the degradation of our natural inheritance knows no borders. The greater the conformity to environmental protection laws that are shared between countries, the greater the benefits to all of humanity. Democracy, understood in this way, is a threat to the survival of the world. It is irrational, destructive and 'populist'.

This is a variant on the neo-Confucian theories propagated by China which argue that a long-term policy pursued by mandarins and insulated from short-term political considerations achieves far greater outcomes than democracy can allow.[10] Democratic sovereignty, in this view, is an attempt to cheat on global duties, exploits co-operation in the name of individual advantage and sabotages progress. The human rights approach presents a similar argument: that there are absolute constraints on the power of the state to violate the dignity of the human person, irrespective of nationality. There are legitimate constraints on democracy.

This is the moral argument, but it is also re-enforced by sanctions and exclusion. Capital will abandon a country if it does not accommodate its interests. You might say that the history of the past 300 years has been an extended battle between politics and markets as to the limits of the sovereignty of either money or democracy. The abandonment of agreed environmental protections is also to run the risk of exclusion from trade agreements. Co-operation between nations is required and leads to beneficial constraints on sovereignty.

The argument against this is based on a combination of diversity, democracy and equality. There is an enormous pressure of homogenization, of the emptying out of politics and distinct forms of organization within the framework of shared legal and procedural norms. A class of managers, outside of accountability to the people they rule, enforce the same system on everyone and the possibility of resisting that is excluded by Treaty Law. Capitalism becomes eternal and unchallengeable. In that way, foreign policy directly constrains domestic politics. The pressure to conform to universal rules voids society of any distinctive content, and the economy of different forms. The possibility of self-government is only permitted within constraints that render it meaningless. The Treaty requirements within the EU concerning competition and state aid, or in relation to the four freedoms, make resistance to capitalism illegal. They limit the power of workers to negotiate, of local authorities to support business or the state to pursue an industrial policy. Owing to the constant pressure of commodification that capitalism exerts, they delegitimate the democratic process as a sham and open up the space for an ugly and aggressive nationalism as the only alternative. A similar process was at work in inter-war Europe in relation to the gold standard.[11]

The EU morphed from a substantive economic partnership at its inception to a globalizing behemoth. This is not sustainable. It either moves into a full political union, with the redistribution that requires, or it will remain unstable and prone to disintegration. Britain must champion the goals of the EU, peace, prosperity and democracy in Europe as a matter of mutual interest, and pursue these with all the member states, in both bilateral arrangements and agreements with the EU. The economic degradation of the South European countries through their inability to devalue their currency and the dynamics of Eastern Europe can be mediated by an alternative alliance of nation states, bound by mutual protection in terms of security, workers' organizations and environmental legislation.

139

It is in the areas of peace, the environment and labour that Britain must play a leading role in brokering an alliance of democratic European states. Internationalism rather than globalization is the organizing principle.

We could broker a coalition of islands that are threatened by rising sea levels and fears of continental domination. Hong Kong, Taiwan and Japan are islands in fear of Chinese domination and ecological eviscera-tion.[12] New Zealand, the West Indies and Sri Lanka are islands with links to the wider Commonwealth with distinctive island cultures and mutual concerns. The rediscovery of our national history as an island requires the rediscovery of other islands with which we share interests and threats.

We need to renew the substantive meaning of the Commonwealth as a civic and trading association built around the liberties and democracy. A post-colonial approach would be the recognition of this alliance as reciprocal and based on non-domination. A shared com-mitment to democratic Parliamentary self-government, the common law and freedom of association are the core institutions and practices that characterize this realm.

Nigeria and South Africa are both members, and it is here that the new civic alliances should be built around universities, the civil service, trade unions and religious freedoms. The Commonwealth offers African countries an alternative to Chinese domination, which is extrac-tive and instrumental. A covenantal approach to nature, the liberties and mutual protection would characterize this alliance. Land reform and democracy would enable countries to pursue their own ends. There is a great deal of writing about civilizational states that are the basis of a new imperialism, such as China, Iran and India.

The response to this is civic alliances that can resist the domination of large states and corporations as the basis of democracy.

The Iraq War has decimated our sense of interests and obligations in the Middle East. Now that oil is far less significant as a natural resource and significantly cheaper, it is necessary to recognize that Salafist Islam, in its conception of religious purity and the sacred role of violence, is essentially fascist. The two groups within both Iraq and Syria who fought against ISIS were the Kurds and the Arab Shia. They fought for their own lives, but we also fought with them in order to defeat the Caliphate, and that should be acknowledged and form the basis of our alliances within the region.

The Kurdish resistance in Syria is particularly important. When ISIS burst over the border into Iraq and captured all the military equipment donated by the United States and Britain, they took all before them as the Iraqi Army disintegrated. The resistance to this in Syria was led by the Kurdish PYD, which established a form of local democracy, based on local councils, with equality of women's representation in both civic and military structures. It offers a model of a democratic society in pluralist countries based on mutual interests and practices. Within the self-governing area of Rojava, it has brought Sunni Arabs, Assyrian Christians, Turkmen as well as Kurds into a common self-governing framework, which has been resilient in the face of both ISIS and Turkish aggression. In their development of the civic, political and military institutions required to sustain their achievements, they are natural allies within the region. They are modest, local partners, as is appropriate to our status and ethics. As the United States

141

retreats, the people of Eastern Syria could be abandoned to Turkish, Russian and Iranian subjugation. It is vital that we build upon the existing military relationship, established during the fight against ISIS, and establish a durable alliance. Post-colonial foreign policy is based on mutual interests, practices and alliances, and the Kurds of Rojava offer all those things.

In Iraq, the system established after the invasion has been prey to sectarian politics, Iranian domination, corruption and maladministration. Both Iraqi Kurds and Shia are no longer directly oppressed by the minority Sunni community, but the emerging form of government is being rejected, particularly by the Shia against Shia rule, on the grounds of corruption, tyranny and violence. The protests that began in Baghdad and Basra in 2019 were explicitly in opposition to corruption, violence and the chronic condition of public services. More than 500 protesters have been killed by Iranian-backed militias. And still they protest and the assassinations continue. In this case, as with the Kurds in Syria, the Iraqi Shia have not only defeated ISIS, they have refused to accept authoritarian communitarian domination. They assert a different conception of accountability, democracy and justice. They have rejected the system we imposed, based on confessional representation, and wish to uphold the liberties and forms of democratic accountability. The Iraq War did break a tyrannical system but had no conception of what to replace it with. The possibilities are there to redeem that by supporting a non-corrupt civil service, autonomous universities, self-governing cities, free and democratic trade unions and freedom of religion, association, conscience and expression. These are the explicit demands of the protesters and they are our natural allies.

As the organizing principle of its foreign policy, Labour should make free and democratic trade unions a condition of any trade deal and build its alliances around that commitment. That gets to the heart of what globalization has been about and allows the traditions of different nations and societies to find expression by rejecting the global system based on the alliance of capital with an administrative state and the degradation of society, workers, liberty and democracy.

Workers of the world unite, you have nothing to lose but your supply chains!

Notes

Introduction

1 G.D.H. Cole, *Labour in the Commonwealth* (London, 1918). R.H. Tawney, *Religion and the Rise of Capitalism* (London, 1922), p. 145.
2 Terry McCarthy, *The Great Dock Strike* (London, 1988). The banners in this book tell the story.

Chapter 1 What's Going On?

1 See Yuri Slezkine, *The Jewish Century* (Princeton, 2006).
2 Tony Blair, speech to Labour Party Conference, September 2005. These sentiments were echoed by President Xi in his foundational speech on socialism with Chinese characteristics: 'History looks kindly on those with resolve, with drive and ambition, and with plenty of guts; it won't wait for the hesitant, the apathetic, or those shy of a challenge.' Xi Jinping, speech to Chinese Communist Party Congress, October 2017.
3 Antonio Gramsci, *Quaderni del carcere*, vol. II (Turin, 1930), pp. 33–4.
4 See Sam Quinones, *Dreamland* (London, 2015).

5 For the decline in the returns to labour across all western economies, see ILO and OECD, 'The Labour Share in G20 Economies' (Antalya, 2015).

6 Pierre Manent, 'Repurposing Europe', *First Things* (April 2016).

7 G.K. Chesterton, *Orthodoxy* (New York, 2004), p. 86.

8 See Richard Tuck, *The Left Case for Brexit* (Cambridge, 2020).

9 Chris Bickerton, *From Member States to Nation States* (Oxford, 2012).

10 See chapter 4.

11 See chapter 5.

12 John Hoskyns and Norman Strauss, *Stepping Stones*, Centre for Policy Studies (London, November 1977). This is perhaps the most significant think tank document ever written.

13 See Nick Land, *Shanghai Basics* (Beijing, 2010).

14 Michel J. Crozier, Samuel P. Huntington and Joji Watanuki, *The Crisis of Democracy: Report on the Governability of Democracies to the Trilateral Commission* (New York, 1975), p. 13.

15 Ronald Butt, 'Economics are the Method: The Object is to Change the Soul', *Sunday Times*, 3 May 1981.

16 Anthony Giddens, *The Transformation of Intimacy: Sexuality, Love and Eroticism in Modern Societies* (Cambridge, 1992).

17 Ulrich Beck and Elisabeth Beck-Gernsheim, *Individualization, Institutionalized Individualism and Its Social and Political Consequences* (London, 2002).

18 Philip Gould, *The Unfinished Revolution: How the Modernisers Saved the Labour Party* (London, 1999).

19 Robert B. Reich, *The Work of Nations: Preparing Ourselves for 21st Century Capitalism* (New York, 1992), p. 41.

20 See chapter 5.

21 Mervyn King, Edinburgh business speech, 19 October 2009.

Chapter 2 The Meaning of Socialism

1 Bernard Crick, *In Defence of Politics* (London, 1962), p. 32.
2 Alasdair MacIntyre, 'Epistemological Crisis, Dramatic Narrative and the Philosophy of Science', *The Monist*, vol. 60, no. 4, October 1977, pp. 453–72.
3 See chapter 3.
4 See M.B. Reckitt and C.E. Bechhofer, *The Meaning of National Guilds* (London, 1918).
5 See Michael Lind, *The New Class War: Saving Democracy from the Metropolitan Elite* (Penguin, 2020).
6 Jeremiah 29: 7 (New King James Version).
7 See chapter 5.
8 Aristotle, *The Politics*, 1275a (20–9) and 1267b (1).
9 See R.H. Tawney, *The Radical Tradition* (London, 1964).
10 Karl Polanyi, *The Great Transformation: The Political and Economic Origins of Our Time* (Boston, 1944).
11 Ibid., p.72.
12 English football is an example of this. Despite the intensity of commodification, football clubs are not simply commodities.
13 For internal goods see Alasdair MacIntyre, *After Virtue* (Notre Dame, 1981).
14 Polanyi, *The Great Transformation*, p. 162.
15 'The organization of labor is only another term for the forms of life of the common people.' Polanyi, *The Great Transformation*, p. 75.
16 Ibid., p. 178.
17 Ibid., p. 195.
18 Ibid., p. 42.
19 The Lisbon Treaty is a good example of this.

20 Polanyi, *The Great Transformation*, p. 140.

21 Karl Polanyi, 'The Economy as Instituted Process' in Mark Granovetter and Richard Swedberg (eds), *The Sociology of Economic Life* (third edition; New York, 2018), pp. 3–21,

22 Polanyi, *The Great Transformation*, p. 34.

23 Ibid., p. 70.

24 See Giovanni Arrighi, *The Long Twentieth Century* (London, 1993), pp. 183–95.

25 John Clare, 'The Mores' (1820).

26 Polanyi, *The Great Transformation*, p. 40.

27 Ibid., p. 149.

28 See Arrighi, *The Long Twentieth Century*, p. 267.

29 Which employed Polanyi when he fled from Hungary. See Jonathan Rose, *The Intellectual Life of the British Working Class* (New Haven, CT, 2010).

30 See J.G.A. Pocock, *The Ancient Constitution and the Feudal Law* (Cambridge, 1987).

31 Polanyi, *The Great Transformation*, p. 142.

32 Ibid., p. 237. The parallel with the euro and the European Central Bank is instructive today.

33 'Intellectually, this myth represented the triumph of economic rationalism and, inevitably, an eclipse of political thought.' Karl Polanyi, *The Livelihood of Man*, ed. Harry W. Pearson (New York, 1977), p. 14.

34 Max Weber, *The Russian Revolutions*, trans. and ed. Gordon C. Wells and Peter Baehr (Cambridge, 1995), p. 103.

35 Karl Marx, 'The Eighteenth Brumaire of Napoleon Bonaparte', in *Later Political Writings*, ed. and trans. Terrell Carver (Cambridge, 1996), p. 32.

Chapter 3 From Contract to Covenant

1 The Chinese model, along with South Korea and Japan, are examples of where the state has been a central actor in the organization of the economy. As export-based economies, they worked within the price system externally but within their national borders they pursued an industrial strategy that worked outside that constraint.

2 See Andrew Haldane, 'The Doom Loop', *London Review of Books*, vol. 34, 2012, pp. 21–2.

3 See Christian Dartmann, *Re-distribution of Power, Joint Consultation or Productivity Coalition? Labour and Postwar Reconstruction in Germany and Britain, 1945–1953* (Bochum, 1996).

4 See also Wolfgang Streeck, *Buying Time* (London, 2016).

5 *Financial Times*, 19 January 2015. See also Office of National Statistics, 'Labour Market Overview, UK', 15 January 2022.

6 Alasdair MacIntyre, *After Virtue* (Notre Dame, IN, 1981), p. 191.

7 See Davide Arcidiancono et al., *Foundational Economy* (Manchester, 2018).

8 See Giovanni Dosi, 'Sources, Procedures and the Micro-economic Effects of Innovation', *Journal of Economic Literature*, vol. 26, 1988, pp. 1120–71.

9 Mark Elam, 'Markets, Morals and the Powers of Innovation', *Economy and Society*, vol. 22, no. 1, 1993, pp. 1–41.

10 Ibid., p. 3. See also Wolfgang Streeck, 'Productive Constraints: On the Institutional Conditions of Diversified Quality Production', in Streeck, *Social Institutions and Economic Performance: Studies of Industrial Relations in Advanced Capitalist Economies* (London, 1992), pp. 1–40.

11 For the development of some of the concepts used

here, see J.C. Nyiri and Barry Smith (eds), *Practical Knowledge: Outlines of a Theory of Tradition and Skills* (London, 1988). See also Stephen Turner, *The Social Theory of Practices: Tradition, Tacit Knowledge and Presuppositions* (Chicago, 1994).

12 See Wolfgang Streeck, 'Beneficial Constraints: On the Economic Limits of Rational Voluntarism', in J. Rogers Hollingsworth and Robert Boyer (eds), *Contemporary Capitalism: The Embeddedness of Institutions* (Cambridge, 1997), pp. 197–219.

13 Paul Hirst and Jonathan Zeitlin, 'Flexible Specialisation v. Post-Fordism: Theory, Evidence and Policy Implications', *Economy and Society*, vol. 20, no.1, 1991, p. 11.

14 An excellent analysis of the different types of economy that makes this distinction between formal and substantive through the idea of a foundational economy of material and providential goods is Luca Calafati et al., 'Building Foundational Britain: From Paradigm Shift to New Political Practice', *Renewal*, vol. 27, no. 2, 2019, pp. 13–23.

15 See chapter 2 on Polanyi.

16 See Karel Williams et al., *The End of the Experiment? From Competition to the Foundational Economy* (Manchester, 2014). See also Andrew G. Haldane, Chief Economist, Bank of England, 'Productivity Puzzles', speech, London School of Economics, 20 March 2017, https://www.bankofengland.co.uk/speech/2017/productivity-puzzles.

17 See Margaret Ackrill and Leslie Hannah, *Barclays: The Business of Banking* (Cambridge, 2001), pp. 320–60.

18 See Federico Mor, 'Bank Rescues of 2007–09: Outcome and Costs', *Briefing Paper 5748*, House of Commons Library, 8 October 2018.

19 'Corporate Governance Reform' Green Paper, 2016, p. 18.

20 Ibid., p. 16.

21 Franklin Allen and Douglas Gale, *Comparing Financial Systems* (Cambridge, MA, 2000). See also Andrew G. Haldane, 'Who Owns a Company?', University of Edinburgh Corporate Finance Conference, 22 May 2015, p. 3.

22 John Asker, Allan Collard-Wexler and Jan De Loecker, 'Dynamic Inputs and Resource (Mis)Allocation', *Journal of Political Economy*, vol. 122, 2014, pp. 1013–63.

23 See Haldane, 'Who Owns a Company?'

24 Piergiorgio Alessandri and Andrew G. Haldane, 'Banking on the State', speech delivered at the Federal Reserve Bank of Chicago, 6 November 2009, https://www.bankofengland.co.uk/speech/2009/banking-on-the-state.

25 Gregory Jackson and Igor Filatotchev, 'Financing, Business Strategy, Corporate Governance and the Growth of Medium-Sized Business: An Exploratory Comparison of the UK and Germany', The Centre for Business Performance, August 2009. See also Carsten M. Jungmann, 'The Effectiveness of Corporate Governance in One-Tier and Two-Tier Board Systems – Evidence from the UK and Germany', *European Company and Financial Law Review*, vol. 3, no. 4, 2007, pp. 426–74.

26 Stephen C. Smith, 'On the Economic Rationale for Co-determination Law', *Journal of Economic Behavior & Organization*, vol. 16, 1991, pp. 261–81.

Chapter 4 Democratic Renewal

1 See Jon Cruddas, *The Dignity of Labour* (Cambridge, 2020).

2 See John P. McCormick, *Machiavellian Democracy* (Cambridge, 2011), pp. 83–4.

3 In this, a variety of abuse and neglect were perpetuated for decades. There was widespread knowledge of it yet no means to effect change.

Chapter 5 Internationalism versus Globalization

1 The Conservatives increased their vote in seats with high numbers of voters without degrees on lower than average wages. Matthew Goodwin and Oliver Heath, *Low-Income Voters, the 2019 Election and the Future of British Parties*, Rowntree Trust, June 2020, pp. 7–10.

2 See Maurice Glasman, *Unnecessary Suffering* (London, 1995), chapter 3.

3 See ibid., chapter 2.

4 See Paul Blusten, *Schism: China, America, and the Fracturing of the Global Trading System* (Montreal, 2019). Bob Davis and Lingling Wei, *Superpower Showdown: How the Battle between Trump and Xi Threatens a New Cold War* (New York, 2020). Michael Lind, *The New Class War: Saving Democracy from the Metropolitan Elite* (New York, 2020).

5 National Bureau of Asian Research, 'Harmonic Convergence: China and the Right to Development', August 2020.

6 ILO and OECD, 'The Labour Share in G20 Economies' (Antalya, 2015).

7 James D. Rice, *Tales from a Revolution: Bacon's Rebellion and the Transformation of Early America* (Oxford, 2012).

8 John J. Mersheimer, *The Great Delusion: Liberal Democracy and International Relations* (New Haven, CT, 2018).

9 Glasman, *Unnecessary Suffering*, pp. 59–65.

10 Peter Bol, *Neo-Confucianism in History* (Cambridge, MA, 2008).

11 Karl Polanyi, *The Great Transformation: The Political and Economic Origins of Our Time* (Boston, 1944), chapter 3.

12 See J.G.A. Pocock, *The Discovery of Islands: Essays in British History* (Cambridge, 2005).

Index

accountability
  democracy 101
  leaders of institutions and
    115
Alinsky, Saul 109
Amazon.com
  employment practices 130–1
  tech oligarchy of 59
Anti-Corn-Law Bill 50
Apple, tech oligarchy of 59
Apprenticeship Laws 52
Aquinas, Thomas 2
Arcidiancono, Davide 77–8
Aristotle
  assumptions about good 36
  ethics 2, 32
  the Good Life 5–6, 44–5
  politics and money 44–5
  we are political beings 34
association, freedom of 9, 34
  China and 130
  common life 55
  criminalization of 9
  globalization and 121
  internationalism 124
  socialism and 54

  strength of the weak 32
  trade unions and 4
Attlee, Clement 105
Austria, collapse of currency,
    53

Bangladesh 136
Bank Act of 1834 50
banks see finance and financial
    institutions
Banks of England
  corporations 94
  regional charter 86–8
Barclays Bank, 2008 crash and
    86
Beck, Ulrich, individualization
    and 24–5, 28
Belgium
  collapse of currency 53
  disintegrating left 15
Bevin, Ernest
  internationalism 124
  post-war Germany and 72
  view of EU 105
Blair, Tony
  China and 127

Index

on global order 14–15
liberal political settlement 27
the Third Way 25
Blatchford, Robert 7
Blue Labour
  basis of 107–8
  birth of 1–4, 10
  communities and pluralism 34–8
  goals of 59–61
  internationalism 43, 44
  mutuality and 38
  political community of 56–7
  traditions of 2, 32–3
  West German economy and 72
Bolshevism *see* communism
Booth, William 9
Brazil 15
Brexit
  civic ecology and 99–101
  class coalitions 120
  Conservatives and 95
  coronavirus and 97–8
  Labour shift and 30
  leading to 15, 21
  meaning of 103–5
  universities and 131
Britain
  1931 collapse of currency 53
  change of era 120–2
  Chinese technology and 125–6
  City of London 82–3
  common law and Parliament 37
  Commonwealth and 140
  Commonwealthmen movement 6
  compared to Germany 71
  corporate governance 89–92
  divisions in 13–15
  foreign policy goals 121
  freeborn 32
  global/domestic finances 81–8
  House of Lords 112
  manufacturing 82
  maritime trade 83–4, 121
  national interest as finance 121
  Norman Conquest 52
  Parliament and 3, 112–14
  Poor Laws 102
  regional development 86–8
  right wing and China 127
  rights of freeborn 6–7
  in transition 16
  Tudor/Stuart economy 49–50
Brown, Gordon
  job predictions 74–5
  Labour electoral loss 29
  saving banks 2
Burke, Edmund 33

Cameron, David 127
capitalism
  assumptions of 43
  Catholic critique of 32
  centralizing ownership 85
  commodification by 19
  creative power of 106
  democracy and 137
  destructive power of 62–3, 106
  ideology of globalization 18–20
  labour representation in 71
  Labour understanding of 6
  money dominates labour 44–5, 122–5, 126–9

capitalism (*cont.*)
  nations and loyalty 138–9
  power of money 108
  rewards selfishness 40
  social partnership 132
  see also commodification;
    corporations; finance and
    financial institutions
care and carers financialized 43
Castle, Barbara 105
Catholic social thought 2
  Blue Labour traditions 32
  the common good 40
  social relationships 44
  workers' rights and 7–8
Chartist movement 60
Chesterton, G.K. 17
China
  communism and 133
  coronavirus and 129–30
  global economy and 16, 63,
    123, 126–9
  human rights and 129
  International Labour
    Organization 130
  neo-Confucianism 138
  repression under 128–31
  technology 125–6
  United States and 125,
    136–7
  Western right wing and
    127
choice
  as freedom 11
  obligations and 33
Christianity
  defending humans 51
  New Labour and 12–13
  workers 37
  see also Catholic social
    thought

Citizens UK 109
civic ecology 87–8
  globalization and 99–101
Clare, John 50
class
  British politics and 98
  cultural taste 27
  identity politics and 24
  solidarity and 31
  see also working class
Clinton, Hillary R., 'basket of
  deplorables' 14
Clinton, William J. (Bill)
  China and 127
  New Democrats 25
Co-operative Society burials
  9–10, 107
Cole, G.D.H. 6, 7
commodification
  Blue Labour and 107
  corporations and 88–9
  defined 45
  fictions 46, 48, 51, 67, 79
  Germany and 71
  privatization and 59
  protection from 58
  resistance to 36, 39, 41, 51,
    101
common good
  Aristotelian idea of 5–6
  corporations and 92–4
  covenant with economy 64
  House of Commons and 7
  individual and state 73
  institutions and 42
  politics of 38–40, 106–8
  religion and workers 7–8
  shared assumptions about
    36
common law
  human labour and 3

Index

idea of covenant 64
Parliament and 37
Commonwealth 140
communism
  China and 133
  decline of 21, 136
communitarianism 55, 56
community/communities
  Blue Labour and 32
  common conversations 36
  the common good 38–40
  coronavirus and 96
  estranged 42
  globalization and 98–100
  international law and 18
  organizing 108–11
  pluralism and difference
    34–8
  role of organizing in 20–1
conscience, freedom of 4, 34,
  121
Conservative Party
  2008 crash leads to 95
  2019 victory and class 98
  Apollo and Mercury 14
  Brexit and 103–4
  capitalism and 118–19
  wins working-class vote
    15–16
contracts, economic activity
  of 70
Corbyn, Jeremy
  policies of 29–30
  view of EU 105
coronavirus pandemic
  China and 129–30
  impact of 96–8
  intensified conditions and
    133
  post-globalization and 125
  virtual world and 132

corporations
  Chinese communism and
    corporatism 133
  EU and 118
  globalization and governance
    88–94
  restoration of 92–4
  risk shifting 91–2
  science and rationality 132
  subcontracting of workers
    128
  US dominance 136–7
  West Germany governance
    and 124–5
Crick, Bernard 35
Crozier, Michel 23

democracy
  accountability and 41
  Blue Labour traditions 32
  changing politics 15
  defeat and 35
  economic 3
  globalization and 16
  human rights and 138
  internationalism 4, 124
  Labour Party and 96, 100–1
  local 3, 99–100, 115–17
  market economics and 27,
    137
  meaning of 34, 101–3
  national politics and 40–3
  Parliament and statecraft
    112–14
  pluralism and difference
    34–8
  resisting money-power 45
  self-government 55–8, 99
  self-organized society 121
  socialism and 54, 57
  solidarity and 2

Index

democracy (*cont.*)
  treaty law and 18
  the tribunes 114–15
Deng Xiaoping 129
Discourses (Machiavelli) 40
*A Dissertation on the Poor
  Laws* (Townsend) 50

East London Communities
  Organization 109, 112
economics
  2008 crash 82, 95
  as autonomous sphere 24
  basic workings of 62
  civic ecology 87–8
  corporations over nations 17
  covenant with 63–5
  democratic 3
  detached from politics 17
  formal and substantive 48
  foundational 77–8, 84
  German social model 71–7
  governance of 62–3, 65–7,
    70, 80–1
  Hayek's catalaxy 68
  household debt 27
  Keynesian 73, 98
  maritime 8–9
  market exchange 73
  market forces 9
  market storms 48–51, 59,
    70
  'market utopianism' 46–9
  monopolies and 59
  New Right critique 123
  non-market institutions 54
  Polanyi on 68–71
  politics and the market
    53–4
  post-war settlement 22, 24
  price and wage control 24
  requires institutions 45
  as self-regulating system
    47–8
  Speenhamland model 50
  stagnation 23–4
  three activities of 70
  see also capitalism; finance
    and financial institutions;
    globalization; knowledge
    economy; liberalism,
    economic; socialism
education
  apprenticeships 9, 76, 84
  Tudor guilds 49–50
  universities and 131
  vocational 75–9, 94
Elam, Mar, on expertise 79
elites, member statism 18
*Enterprise, Skills and
  Innovation* (Labour White
  Paper) 26
environment and nature
  commodification of 65, 66
  common good 57
  fictitious commodification of
    19, 46, 50
  human dependence on 45
  local place 99–100
  parish level and 116
  sea level rise 140
  stewardship of 2
  subordination of 132
  supply chains and 133
  without borders 137–8
ethics and virtue 14
European Central Bank 97
European Union (EU)
  coronavirus and 96–7
  Eastern bloc intake 27
  evolution of 26
  free movement and 137

Index

globalization and 73, 120, 139–40
liberal proceduralism 95
Lisbon Treaty 17, 26, 30, 96–7, 105
Maastricht Treaty 17, 26, 30
shift in Labour attitudes 131
social democracy 118–19
expression, freedom of 4, 34, 121

Fabian Society 12
Facebook, tech oligarchy of 59
Fascism, rise of 52–4
finance and financial institutions
2008 crash 82, 85–8
Banks of England 81–8
British national interest and 121
Brown on saving 2
crisis ends Labour success 28
debt of workers 74
domination of 1
German banks 71
high rewards of 85
maritime trade 83–4
payday lending 74
West Germany and 124–5
Foot, Michael 105
France
collapse of currency 53
disintegrating left 15
Francis, Pope on change of era 120
freedom see liberty/freedom
friendly societies 52

Germany
collapse of currency 53
corporations 92–3
post-war 72

Schroeder's Hartz reforms 125
social economy model 71–7
vocational/artisan sector 79
West German economy 124–5
Giddens, Anthony
accelerating modernity 24
unpicking association ties 28
globalization
Brexit and 98–101, 104
capital over labour 122–5
China and 63, 126–9
community and 98–100
consequences of 11–16
coronavirus and 97
corporate governance 17, 27, 88–94
disintegration of 125–31
EU and 73, 120
homogenization of 58
ideology of 18–20
internationalism and 43, 134–43
Labour Party embraces 96
new era of 95–6
New Labour and 1, 28
the parish and 116–17
resistance to 15, 16
the Third Way 25–6
see also internationalism
good, common see common good
Good Life, Aristotelian idea of 5–6
Google, tech oligarchy of 59
Gould, Philip, *The Unfinished Revolution* 25
Gramsci, Antonio on interregnums 16

Index

The Great Transformation
   (Polyani) 45–51
Green Paper on Corporate
   Governance Reform (2016)
   89

Hackney Council 1
Haldane, Andrew
  'doom loop' 67
  on risk shifting 91
Hayek, Friedrich 67–8
Healey, Denis 105
Hemingway, Ernest 10
Hirst, Paul 79–80
history
  change of era 120–2
  Polyani's theory of 46–8
  wrong side of 131–4
Hobbes, Thomas, *Leviathan*
  50
Hobson, S.J. 7
Hong Kong 129, 140
Huawei 125
human beings
  commodification of 19, 50,
   66
  egoism vs altruism 39
  human capital 65–6, 70–1,
   74
  sociability 45
  treated as ends 33
  voracious desires 44–5
human rights
  democracy and 138
  resistance to 15
Hungary 15
Huntington, Samuel 23

identity politics 24
immigration
  Eastern EU intake 27

faith and organization
  109–10
globalization and 20
labour and 131
Labour Party and 106
imperialism, land reform and
  democracy 140–1
India 15
individualism
  Beck on 24–5
  over society 17
  reciprocity as self-interest
   69–70
  and state 73
  statism and 46–7
industrialization
  commodification of labour
   51
  English labour and 50
inequalities *see* poverty and
  inequality
innovation, expertise and 78
institutions
  civil 21, 58
  common good and 42, 57
  community organization 108
  co-operative tradition 108
  decentralized 103
  economics requires 45–6
  educational 73
  between individuals and
   states 46–7
  mutual interest societies 52
  resisting commodification
   51, 68–71
  between state and economy
   68–70
  traditions of 33
insurance mutuals 52
International Labour
  Organization 124

Index

International Monetary Fund 124

internationalism
  constitutional liberalism and 43
  defined 43
  democratic nations 4
  development of 123–4
  vs globalization 134–43
  globalization and 21, 43
  labour and 43, 44, 133
  Labour and 119
Iran, China and 125
Iraq, war and ISIS 141–2
ISIS, fight against 141–2
Islam, Salafist 141

Jeremiah 39

Kant, Immanuel, people as ends and 33
King, Mervyn on 2008 crisis 28
knowledge economy 11
  expertise 78–81
  job predictions 74–5
  sharing 80
  see also education
Kurds 116, 141–2

labour
  apprenticeships 76
  aspects of vocation 77
  capital over 122–5
  China and 133
  corporate representation 71
  creative/knowledge economy 75
  dignity of 2, 31, 97–8, 109–10
  diminishing status of 128

  dominated by capitalism 126–9
  English guilds 49–50
  expertise 78–81
  as fictional commodity 46
  freedom of association 124
  globalization and 11
  human status of 3, 65–6, 70–1, 132, 133
  immigrant 131
  internationalism 123–4
  Labour White Paper on 26
  mutual self-help 52
  organization of 108
  pandemic workers 97–8
  precariats 128
  religion and workers' movement 7–8
  subcontracted 128
  vocational education 75–9
  West Germany and 124–5
  working hours 52
  see also pay and wages; trade unions
Labour Party and movement
  agency for working class 41–2
  ancient roots of 32–3
  Brexit and 100–1, 104–5
  as 'broad church' 13
  capitalist modernity 12
  Catholic and Protestant workers 36
  defection from 75
  Enterprise, Skills and Innovation White Paper 26
  EU and 131
  fundamental tenets of 3
  haunted by working class 21
  internationalism 21, 124

Index

Labour Party and movement
(*cont.*)
  paradoxes of 4
  post-war settlement 122–3
  shift from tradition 95–6
  social democracy and
    118–19
  traditions of 3–10, 58–61,
    113–14
  working class abandons
    15–16
  working-class roots 2–3
  see also Blue Labour; New
    Labour
law
  international vs democratic
    18
  personal rights 7
  sovereignty of 101
  see also common law
League of Nations 124
Leviathan (Hobbes) 50
liberalism, economic
  commodification and 31
  commodification of labour
    51
  Conservative Party and 27
  definition and effects 19–20
  New Democrats 25
  United States and 134
liberalism, social
  New Democrats 25
liberty/freedom
  Blue Labour 57
  choice as 11
  common law 43
  common life 55
  of discussion 61
  four freedoms 4, 121
  four liberties 34
Living Wage campaign 109–11

local democracy 3, 115–17
  environment and 99–100
London Dock Strike (1899)
  8–9

Machiavelli, Niccolò
  Discourses 40
  The Prince 101–2, 114–15
MacIntyre, Alasdair
  ethics 2
  virtue and vocation 77
Manent, Pierre 17
Manning, Cardinal John Henry
  9
manufacturing in Britain 82
Mao Zedong 129
Marx, Karl and Marxism
  fallacies and insights 25
  on tradition 60
member statism 18
Miliband, Ed 29
Mises, Ludwig von 67
modernity
  capitalist 12
  money markets 55–6
  vocation and 77
monarchy and republicanism 4
money/currency
  early twentieth-century
    collapse 53
  as fictional commodity 46
  gold standards 52–3
Morris, William 7
multiculturalism, resistance to
  15

nation states
  Brexit and 104
  coronavirus and 96–7
  corporations and 17, 27
  globalization and 43, 121

Index

governance of economy 26,
62–3, 80–1
individuals and 73
'market utopianism' 46–9
Parliament and statecraft
112–14
Polanyi on 68–71
National Health Service,
creation of 1, 97
nationalism 15
nationalization
Corbyn's policies 30
'doom loop' 67
post-war Labour 72
NATO *see* North Atlantic
Treaty Organization
(NATO)
natural world *see* environment
and nature
Netflix, tech oligarchy of 59
New Labour
accepts globalization 63
China and 127
Corporate Governance Act
91
economic policy 28–9
response to New Right 21
revolutionary approach
12–15
twilight of 1
working-class disenchantment
with 28
New Right ideology 22–4
New Zealand 140
Newcastle United Football Club
85–6
Nigeria 140
Nixon, Richard, China and
127
North Atlantic Treaty
Organization (NATO) 124

Northern Rock, 2008 crash
85–8
nuclear energy 126

Osborne, George 127

Pakistan 136
China and 125
parish *see* local democracy
Parliamentary Reform Act of
1982 52
particularity 15
pay and wages
corporate executives 89
debt and 74
living/poverty 80
stagnation 74
peace-seeking 39
Penty, A.J. 7
pluralism and difference 34–8
recognizing difference 106
solidarity and 40
Poland 15
Polanyi, Karl
on commodification 66
The Great Transformation
45–51
historical agency 51
market storms 48–51, 70
rejects statism and market
orders 68–81
theory of history 46–8
politics
Apollo and Mercury 13–14,
27
Aristotle and 44–5
changing consensus 65–7
concerns of the left 96
as conservative 103
corruption and tyranny 137
county and parish 115–17

Index

politics (*cont.*)
  creativity of 33–4
  economics leads 17
  as ethics 35
  instrumentalism and evasion
    40
  Machiavelli and 101–2
  moralistic 14–15, 100
  New Right critique 123
  organizing communities
    108–11
  Parliament and statecraft
    112–14
  power and money 44–5
  relational 102–3
  social democracy 118–19
  subordinated to markets
    53–4
  tribunes 114–15
Poor Laws
  1601 Act 49
  1834 reform 50, 52
  apprenticeship laws 84
poverty and inequality
  basic income model 50
  the common good and 38
  community organization
    111
  household debt 27
  increase of 28
  industrialization and 50
  Tudor/Stuart England 49
power
  balance of 70
  disempowerment 20
  of money 44–5, 62–3, 108
  relational 108
  of state 108
  three kinds of 108
The Prince (Machiavelli) 101–2
  on the tribunes 114–15

privatization
  'doom loop' 67
  of English common lands
    49
  New Right ideology and
    23
  plundering assets 59

race and ethnicity
  property rights 107
  two faces of the United States
    135
radicalist tradition 4
Reagan, Ronald 22
reasoning, money and power
  44–5
reciprocity 55
  economic activity of 70
  principle of society 69–70
  socialism and 57
redistribution
  centralized state and 73
  economic activity of 70
Reich, Robert 25–6
religion
  changing politics 15
  community organization and
    109–10
  freedom of 4, 34, 121
  secularism and 4
  workers and 7–8, 106–7
  see also Catholic social
    thought
republicanism 4
rights
  common law and 43
  democracy and 100–1
  natural law 7
  see also human rights
Roman Empire, founding of
  City of London 82–3

Index

Russia
    Second World War 136
    Soviet disintegration 63

Salvation Army, London Dock
        Strike (1899) and 8–9
Schroeder, Gerhard
    Hartz reforms 125
    the Third Way 25
secularism, resistance to 15
social democracy
    fate of 118–19
    renewing society 56
Social Democratic Federation
    12
social mobility, concept of 104
social partnership 132
social reform, conservativism
        and 4
socialism
    Burkean 37–8
    constituted by society 33–4
    defence of society 54
    democracy and 57
    domesticating capital 63
    guild 7
    market exchange 54
    meaning of 60
    municipal 84
    Parliamentary 7
    planned system 67
    reciprocity 54, 57
    redistribution 54
    sociology of 15
society
    balancing power 70
    'market storms' 48–51
    'market utopianism' 46–9
    socialism and 54
South Africa 140
sovereignty 57

Sri Lanka 140
states see nation states
Statute of Artificers of 1563
        49
Stoke Mandeville Hospital
        115
Syria
    ISIS and 141–2
    local assembly 116–17

Taiwan, China and 129, 140
Tawney, R.H. 6
taxation, excessive 23
technology
    borderless 11
    determinism 18, 43
    oligarchs of 59
    virtual world 132
TELCO 109
Thatcher, Margaret
    China and 127
    effects of policies 123
    ending collectivist society 24
    liberal political settlement
        27
    rise of New Right 22
Third Way
    limitations of 73
    managerialism 106
    progressive globalization
        25–6
    twilight of 1
Tories see Conservative Party
Townsend, Joseph, *A
        Dissertation on the Poor
        Laws* 50
trade
    labour and free trade 79
    maritime 83–4, 122
trade unions
    China and 130

trade unions (*cont.*)
  community organization and
    109
  criminalization 9
  emergence of 52
  freedom of association 4
  institutionalized 22
  London Dock Strike (1899)
    8–9
  marginalized 23
  New Right and 123
  West Germany and 124–5
tribunes 114–15
Trump, Donald 15

Uighur Muslims 129
The Unfinished Revolution
  (Gould) 25
United Nations 124
United States
  Bacon's Rebellion 135
  China and 125, 127
  Clinton and New Democrats
    25
  foreign policy 136–7
  global order and nations 121
  incoherence of policies
    134–7

virtue
  in the economy 69
  good as learned 44
  incentives to 40
  Machiavelli on 101–2
  vocation and 77
vocational education 75–9, 94

Watanuki, Joji 23
Weber, Max 53
Workers' Educational
  Association 51
working class
  Brexit and 104
  historical tradition 3–4
  Labour as agency for 41–2
  Labour Party retreat 96
  Labour roots in 2–3
  pandemic workers and 97–8
  racially inclusive 98
  reclaiming home 61
World Bank 124
World Health Organization
  124, 130
World Trade Organization
  127, 130

Xi Jinping 128–31

Printed and bound by CPI Group (UK) Ltd, Croydon, CR0 4YY

13/04/2025

14656503-0001